MERCY Rising

SIMPLE WAYS TO PRACTICE
JUSTICE AND COMPASSION

AMBER ROBINSON

D1528793

BEACON HILL PRESS
OF KANSAS CITY

ISBN 978-0-8341-2497-4

Printed in the
United States of America

Cover Design: Lindsey Rohner
Inside Design: Sharon R. Page

Library of Congress Cataloging-in-Publication Data

Robinson, Amber, 1977-
   Mercy rising : simple ways to practice justice and compassion / Amber Robinson.
    p. cm.
   Includes bibliographical references (p.   ).
   ISBN 978-08341-24979-4 (pbk.)
   1. Christian women—Religious life. 2. Voluntarism—Religious aspects—Christianity. 3. Christian giving. 4. Christianity and justicie. 5. Compassion—Religious aspects—Christianity. I. Title.
   BV4527.R585 2010
   261.8'32—dc22

                           2010003489

Published in association with Rosenbaum & Associates Literary Agency, Brentwood, Tennessee.

10 9 8 7 6 5 4 3 2 1

CONTENTS

Introduction	5
Part I: Getting Real About Giving	9
1. Why Justice? Why Me?	11
2. Love Thing	23
3. Daily Bread	35
4. At Home	48
Part II: The One Thing I Can Do	67
5. Shopping	69
6. It's Just Business	86
7. Space Invaders	102
8. Away from Home	117
Part III: Reality Check	133
9. Real Mess, Real Rewards	135
10. How Do I Decide?	149
11. Mercy Rising	164
Appendix A	171
Appendix B	177
Appendix C	179
Appendix D	181
Notes	183
Acknowledgments	188

INTRODUCTION

As part of a college course, my class took a field trip to a museum to view Native American artifacts. I remember just one thing clearly from that visit to the museum: two enormous oil canvases of the Grand Canyon, awash with vibrant oranges, reds, purples, and blues. The first painting showed the breaking light of dawn—silver mountain, floating birds, radiant clouds. The second painting showed the same setting, only at sunset, with slinky shadows, sinister birds, a dying stream. My classmates and I stood beneath the pictures in awe, beauty uniting us into silence. Time stopped as the skill of the craftsman cemented our feet to that spot. Emotion danced freely off the wall into our hearts.

How could two pictures of the very same scene evoke such different moods? One jubilant with hope; the other dark with despair.

Today, years later, I still think about those vivid images when I speak with others about ways to invest in the lives of the poor. Many see social justice issues through the dark lens of the second painting: the portrait of the poor—a dying subject, sick and hopeless. How can we readjust our views enough to see the portrait as a beautiful opportunity—vibrant, alive, and growing?

The needs are real. We've seen the pictures and heard the stories—children dying from lack of access to basic nutrition and health care. Human slaves are trafficked in our home cities and around the world. Believers face prison time in east Asia. Racial injustice still festers in America.

"It's not that I don't care—I just don't know what to do" is the heart cry of many American women. Just day-to-day living keeps us on the edge of emotional overload, and it hurts too much to put faces to the victims. Unending media images leave us emotionally disengaged, so we often just skim over the tough questions: *How do I live out caring for the poor when they seem invisible? Can I care for justice when I feel broken and in debt? Is it even possible for my middle-class, exhausted family to do anything meaningful for others?*

5

Or the bigger question: *So what?*

We can't afford more guilt. We can't afford more debt or financial strain. We can't afford to add one more thing to our to-do lists.

Does our involvement matter?

What if you could make the impact you always dreamed of making? What if you had the tools to organize resources and make them easily accessible? What if this were really doable? Could you begin to feel hope that what you have to offer would, indeed, make a difference?

At this time in human history we see endless possibilities in an interconnected world. Through technology we receive a Pakistani's prayer request instantly. We link with a search engine that donates money to charity with each web search. A pharmaceutical company sends an American woman's breast milk to starving babies in Africa. These are just a few of the exciting ideas to jumpstart your search for your *one* thing—your unique passion and a way to give. *Mercy Rising* will help you organize your ideas to focus on what works for you. This book is divided into three sections:

Why? (Getting Real About Giving)

Why justice—why me?
Why do I need to give with love?
Why should I give if I'm afraid?
Why should I give if I don't have enough?
Why will giving turn my life around?

What? (The *One* Thing I Can *Do*)

What fits at home?
What fits in with shopping?
What fits in business?
What is real hospitality?
What should I do away from home?
What is my *one* thing?

How? (Reality Check)

How do I stay motivated?

How do I avoid scams?

How do I pick a charity to partner with?

How do I see where the money goes?

How do I focus my limited time, energy, and resources?

What do you see in the canyon painting of social justice? Do you see guilt large enough to fill up the canyon? Do you see suffering and despair that make you want to turn away? Do you see the past efforts to scale those rocky ledges that have left you tired and broken? Has the sun set on your willingness to try again?

I confess that the darker view is my natural tendency when the going gets tough. I still flounder along, learning every day from my mistakes. And as I set out to help others, I find a better life, and I think I may have been the needy one. I offer food; I receive spiritual life.

I won't say it's easy. The issues are hard and the people are real—real people mean real messes. I carry the baggage of my own messes into my relationships with others. Many times I feel so tired and busy that I don't have the energy to do one more thing. Then God gently reminds me that when I look into the eyes of a child in Indonesia, or my neighbor in Indiana, or my husband across the kitchen table, I'm looking into the face of Christ. And at that moment my view changes—what I thought was the sunset was the sunrise after all, and I catch a glimpse of a front-row vista view of heaven's handiwork.

And mercy rises.

Is not this the kind of fasting I have chosen: to loose the chains of injustice and untie the cords of the yoke, to set the oppressed free and break every yoke? Is it not to share your food with the hungry and to provide the poor wanderer with shelter—when you see the naked, to clothe him, and not to turn away from your own flesh and blood? Then your *light will break forth like the dawn* and your healing will quickly appear; then your righteousness will go before you, and the glory of the LORD will be your rear guard. Then you will call, and the LORD will answer; you will cry for help, and he will say: Here am I. If you do away with the yoke of oppression, with the pointing finger and malicious talk, and if you spend yourselves in behalf of the hungry and satisfy the needs of the oppressed, then your *light will rise in the darkness,* and your *night will become like the noonday.* The LORD will guide you always; he will satisfy your needs in a sun-scorched land and will strengthen your frame. You will be like a well-watered garden, like a spring whose waters never fail (*Isaiah 58:6-11, emphasis added*).

Part I
Getting Real About Giving

Why Justice? Why Me?

*The only ones among you who will be truly happy are those who
will have sought and found how to serve.*
—Albert Schweitzer

Time stops against the cold frame of the X-ray machine. "Can you turn a little to your left?" Fatigue fumbles the simple directions. My mind wanders with the machine's noises.

Click—recent engagement.

Clack—good friends.

Click—college graduation.

Clack—new job.

But something sits deep in my soul. I don't want to stand still long enough to find out what it is. As doctors examine my chest X-rays against the light board, I review frames of my new life against the light of reason. I hear a puzzled voice across the room, "Inconclusive." My thoughts exactly.

The light fades to dark again for a few years. The 60-to-80-hour work weeks blanket my brain in a deep fog. Questions fall silent as chronic physical pain shouts more loudly.

Flashes of insight bounce off my husband's insistence that I stop this pace; I obsessively need to keep moving. He sees destruction to my body; I see disintegrating emotional connection in my marriage.

After another bad spell, I resign to spend the next several months in bed. As I grow sicker, medical science fails me, and more time passes to revolve those pictures in my mind. They don't add up.

Click, clack, click, clack.

Still inconclusive.

Then other images find their way into the slideshow.

Click—growing up among the working rural poor.

Clack—studying and writing on politics in high school.

Click—participating in an inner-city internship in college. Facing complex struggles with practical training. That's me with the crazy hair.

Clack—mentoring teen girls in my early adult years.

Click—writing and supporting an African child through Compassion International, watching her life transform through the photographs and letters we exchanged.

These disjointed shapes danced in living color, sharply focused, unfading despite my best efforts. What did they have to do with me with me now? That service stuff was what all the young people did to "change the world." I have a different life now with responsibilities and very little free time. Let somebody else take care of it.

But after months of the unwieldy slide show in my head, I caved. Fighting my doubts, I began something deeper than a token contribution or holiday project. I dug into the one small thing I was already doing—caring about children who live in poverty. I became a child advocate with Compassion International and started finding sponsors for other waiting children. I agreed, despite physical pain, to work sign-up tables at sponsorship events.

God supplied amazing stamina that allowed me to get through those late-night events. I took my training more seriously and searched to find better, clearer answers to the questions potential sponsors asked. Lying flat on my back in bed, I prayed more earnestly for my sponsored child and for the charity's worldwide request lists. Right away crazy things began to happen.

First, I had the strength the instant I needed it. Second, residual energy washed over the rest of my life. Tasks like laundry, cleaning, and teaching were getting done faster with less pain.

My life didn't fall apart as I expected, and time seemed to multiply. We found new medical treatment from natural therapies that actually helped. On the other hand, I faced spiritual opposition with unexpected force. Wild craziness broke loose in every area of my life from relationships to circumstantial events. I needed to depend on something greater than myself to get things done. Miss Independent now needed the help of others and their prayers.

But this dependence wasn't all bad, as I found comfort and support in this new experiment unlike what I had experienced before. I was still ill enough that any service would have to fit in with my regular activities—doing chores, going shopping, conducting business—with the people in my everyday life. Was there really a way to make this work for the long term? I needed to try.

Around this time friends started asking questions. We were well past youthful idealism, buying homes, starting families, and putting down roots. "What does justice have to do with us? What happens when we see tragedy in the media but don't know what to do as life moves on? How do we start? Is this just for others or for me too?"

I did not have the answers, but I could research creative ways to live justice as a mom, consumer, or businesswoman—things I was already searching for. I started meeting others who were already doing this—women who were changing their lifestyles to find their one thing.

These weren't women with spare time; they were women who were dealing with their own extreme life circumstances. Despite this, they were serving with deep, lasting joy that was contagious. They didn't have hero or saint complexes; they were just using their hobbies, purchases, and lives in a more focused way.

A decade has passed since the chest X-ray. Life is now going full-speed ahead and is busier than ever, like a never-ending video stream. What does your video stream look like? What are your unique challenges? Why add justice to life's load? Surprisingly, aiding those in need is not the heavy load that breaks a back; rather, it is engine fuel to live in the "ordinary" with clarity, order, peace, and joy.

You Mean Help the Poor, Right?

The panhandler is one of the visible faces of poverty. Can we find better ways to help him or her? The starving African child is another haunting reminder. Are there better ways to engage him or her? What do we really know about the people behind these often-exploited images?

Who are the poor? Where do they live? I was surprised to learn that in the United States the fastest growing segment of those living in poverty are in the suburbs (38.5 percent). Our imaginations take us down dark alleys where we hear gunshots, but only six percent of the poor live in an urban ghetto. One third of the poor are married and work full time. Thirteen million children live in poverty.[1]

Why don't we see them? Maybe we're too busy and just don't notice. Maybe they don't get the same media attention that violent crime victims or natural disaster survivors receive.

Global poverty is much more severe than poverty in the United States. The current world food supply is already strained in these fragile economic conditions. What we view through media screens feels as if it's fiction in faraway places, but the tragedy overseas is very real.

There are many types of poverty that include economic, health, environmental, social, educational, and spiritual.[2] When I discuss poverty in this book, I refer to the types or combinations of types that have a physical manifestation. For example, a wealthy American may be spiritually poor but show no outward sign of his or her need. A different person may suffer economic poverty and also have spiritual and health needs. While the wealthy person's need is real, he or she is not suffering injustice, because he or she has access to spiritual and economic resources, but the physically poor person does not have the same resources. When we understand that poverty takes these different forms, we can see that creative, diverse solutions are needed. One remedy does not cure all ailments.

Who Needs Justice?

Those who need justice are often invisible, because the voices of the marginalized in our culture are rarely heard. Look at the following list. There are many groups of people who need our help both in the United States and overseas.

Domestic	Global
Domestic Violence	Domestic Violence
Sex Trafficking	Sex Trafficking
Orphans/Foster Care	Orphans/Orphanages
Widows/Single Moms	Widows/Single Moms
Teen Moms/Unborn Children	Teen Moms/Unborn Children
Neglected/Abused Children	Neglected/Abused Children
Child Abuse	Prenatal Care/Parent Training
Hunger	Hunger
Food Banks/Shelters	World Food Shortage
Homelessness	Homelessness
	Clean Water Access
Prisoners/Families	Martyrs—Imprisoned for Faith
Military Families/Veterans	Religious/Political freedom
Racial/Ethnic Justice	Racial/Ethnic Justice
	Basic Human Rights
Medical Care	Medical Care
Illness	Illness (Malaria/AIDS)
Homebound/Caregivers	Homebound/Caregivers
Special-needs Families	Special-needs Families
Elderly	Elderly
Disaster Relief	Disaster Relief
Environmental Concerns	Environmental Concerns
	Clean Water/Sanitation
Working Poor	Working Poor
Livable Wage	Work Conditions
Literacy/Education	Literacy/Education
Joblessness	Joblessness
Human Trafficking	Human Trafficking

You may already be helping in some of these areas. Maybe you donate to a local food pantry or participate in special giving during holidays. Do you buy produce that's grown locally or fair trade items? If you do any of these, you're living justice every day. But there's still work to be done.

Why Is Justice Important?

What's the big deal after all?

My friend Jo comes to mind. Jo has many attributes. She's fun to be with, joyful, and thoughtful. In fact, it is not easy to separate those inner qualities from my perception of her.

In the same way God has many attributes. He often seems far away because I can't see His face, but I can know His attributes: holiness, love, mercy, grace, and truth. Sometimes it's hard to remember to include justice in that list.

We speak with our lips what's on our hearts. Jo speaks most about family, friends, spiritual things, and photography. Everyone who spends time with her knows that these are the things that are important to her. When God speaks to us through His Word, it seems fair to say that He speaks about what matters to Him.

How many times in Scripture do you think justice issues are mentioned? Ten? One hundred? One thousand? Tony Hall, former United States Ambassador for Humanitarian Issues, says there are more than 2,500 verses in the Bible about justice issues.[3] See the Appendix for a list of some of the key passages.

Not only is justice a part of God's character—it's a central issue repeated more than 2,500 times. If justice is a key attribute of the God we serve, it should be a key attribute of His servants. Is it rare to hear these issues spoken about in mainstream Christian circles, in everyday conversations with friends and family? Why is that? Maybe it's the connotation of the word "justice." Sometimes when I say "justice," people hear "fanatical socialism." You may think of the term "social justice" in this context.

Social Justice or Kingdom Justice?

What is social justice? Social justice is "the distribution of advantages and disadvantages within a society."[4] Others have told me that the term "social justice" brings up images of government programs such as unemployment, welfare, and Social Security. I'm interested in a different society, a different kingdom. I'm interested in an upside-down kingdom. When the terms "justice" or "social justice" are used in these pages, I mean "Kingdom justice."

Society says to claw your way to the top.

Kingdom justice says, "The last shall be first."

Society says to take care of yourself and your family first. If you have anything left, you can give that away.

Kingdom justice seeks first God's agenda and then trusts that all the other stuff will work out.

Society glorifies the wealthy, the brilliant, the famous, the well-bred. Use those connections to win.

Kingdom justice humbles itself to aid those who are oppressed.

Social justice follows the whims of a fickle crowd.

Kingdom justice is an age-old wisdom, never-changing, ever-constant, until one day the Author of justice will return, and every wrong will be righted.

Why Me?

"Compassion is sometimes the fatal capacity for feeling what it is like to live inside somebody else's skin. It is the knowledge that there can never really be any peace and joy for me until there is peace and joy finally for you too" (Frederick Buechner).

Many women have asked, "Why me? I write my contribution check. Isn't that enough?" Those questions rattle inside me as well. Each one of us has a different answer to that kind of question, but here are some basic reasons we must do more.

I Will Recognize Jesus

Ask any Midwesterner about the weather in late winter and, he or she will tell you it's enough to make you bonkers. Our landscape from Valentine's Day to Easter is painted with brown-grey mush mixed with enough sunshine to torment you with scenes from far-away summer. Right around Easter we regain hope. Reluctant living things rise up out of the dead earth. Miracles linger in every bud and bloom. I find myself inspecting every branch and blade of grass. When trees leaf in May, we breathe a sigh of relief—finally. But find me in July with an abundance of green things around me, and I won't even notice the trees. They're still changing and growing, but I'm unaware.

In the same way, the bleak backdrop of poverty and injustice sets the stage that best contrasts God's work. I see and recognize Jesus most in the miraculous resurrection of lives once dismantled.

When asked if He was legitimate, Jesus cited only two items from His résumé. Sick are healed. Good news is preached to the poor (Matthew 11:5-6). When others were thinking, *He doesn't look or act like God,* Jesus was pointing out the new life, the growth in the darkest places.

If we don't interact with the poor, it's too easy to skip over the 2,500 verses, walk past the needy, and skim over Jesus himself.

Jesus Will Recognize Me

What is good activity? Time spent in prayer, church activities, or working on my vices? Those may be worthwhile, but notice what makes Jesus' top six list. In Matthew 25 Jesus forecasts the future. He has the nations gathered before Him. We're all claiming to be His, but He knows better. He separates true followers from the crowd. How? Jesus gives a list that's repeated three times: those who feed the hungry, give water to the parched, clothe the naked, shelter the stranger, nurse the sick, and visit the prisoner. Even as one who advocates for poor children, this list surprises me in its focus on justice. I still don't fully understand how important it is, but I want more than anything for Jesus to recognize me as His.

They Belong to My Family

I had just finished a physical therapy session. I needed to get home and had one last errand to do. On the way there, I saw a woman in distress on the side of the road. A line I had recently read reminded me not to "turn away from your own flesh and blood" (Isaiah 58:7).

I was beginning to groan silently to myself, *I just want to go home.* I drove away but turned around and came back, because I knew I wouldn't drive away if that were my child, sister, cousin, or mother on the road. I would have stopped. Why? *Family.* We do stuff for family that we wouldn't do for anyone else.

Something in me resists connecting to a destitute woman. I don't know why that is, because I understand that Jesus considers me a close family member of His, even though I don't deserve that. In the same way, those who are marginalized by society may not "deserve" family status. A complete stranger can be part of us—part of our family—because he or she is a human being, our flesh and blood.

Imagine for a moment that your daughter is part of the sex-trafficking business. Imagine that your son is starving to death because of poor nutrition. Imagine your elderly mother dying because of the lack of basic sanitation.

Can you visualize not helping? Me neither.

Ketchup and Mustard—Deanna's Story

Our church paper announced weekly opportunities to serve Sunday supper at the local mission. After seeing that insert for a year, I knew what I wanted to do for my 50th birthday. My husband, Jeff, and our three children came along to commemorate the day.

The first Sunday we served I kept busy, too uncomfortable to talk with the men. My daughter, Natalie, and I served desserts. Jeff and our sons, Thomas and Matthew, served from behind the counter. The men were thankful and gracious. Thomas got back to the car and stated, "I want to come back next week."

That's how our service to others began. My family and I stretched ourselves to form relationships with the men in the recovery program. We looked forward to seeing them and hearing about their concerns. I started carrying a little piece of paper and a pen in my pocket to help me remember what to pray for them. Natalie began helping one man memorize his required Bible verses. He knew he would get trouble from her if he didn't toe the line!

One Sunday we had plenty of volunteers, so I told the kitchen leader, "I'm going upstairs to the chapel."

She said, "Wait. I've got a job for you."

She disappeared into the kitchen and returned with ketchup and mustard bottles. She then asked me to stand behind a table and hand out condiments, even though they didn't seem to garnish that particular meal. *What a waste of my time! Come on, Lord—mustard and ketchup? I want something useful to do. I'd be more helpful upstairs playing games!*

As I stood there, I watched the men eat. With their heads bowed over their trays, mechanically spooning food into their mouths, they avoided eye contact. I could see desperation etched deeply into their faces—the desperation that prompts a grown man to stand in line for free food. When I stopped busying myself by being "useful," I saw their brokenness—and my own.

I'm encouraged by the men who have nothing yet still report what the Lord has done for them. They're hungry for relationships and for people in their lives who care enough to remember their names. When one has lost everything, those small things become a lifeline to survival.

On our first Sunday there—my 50th birthday—the leader mentioned that the mission house itself is a common structure, but it *transforms* into a sacred space because Jesus is there. I finally understand what she meant.

Character traits that often elude us are found in abundance among the poor. Those without physical means cultivate love, patience, kindness, and joy in the soil of hard circumstance. I operate under the illusion that *my* hard work puts food on the table, and I forget about the creator and sustainer of the heartbeat in my chest. How many others have helped me out along the way? Identifying with the weak is crucial to spiritual life. They may start as "one of those people" but they soon become "one of us." Our own social, spiritual, and emotional poverty becomes evident only through interaction with the needy.

To see Christ.

To be identified as His.
To help my own flesh and blood
To identify with the weak.
And—to enjoy the rewards.

Limitless Benefits

Bottom line—you have more to gain than to lose.
- Blessing in work (Deuteronomy 15:10)
- Provision in hard times (Proverbs 28:27; Isaiah 58:11)
- Strength (Isaiah 58:11)
- Treasure in heaven (Luke 12:33)
- Impartiality (James 2:2-6)
- Blessings on family (Acts 10:4)
- Healing (Isaiah 58:8)
- Protection (Isaiah 58:8)
- Honor (Psalm 112:9)
- Joy (Isaiah 58:14)

Isaiah 58:14 says, "Then you will find your joy in the LORD, and I will cause you to ride on the heights of the land and to feast on the inheritance of your father Jacob. The mouth of the LORD has spoken."

Joy—it's the most fulfilling part of my life in identifying with the poor. But what if you aren't feeling joyful right now?

Click—heavy guilt.

Clack—wasted time

Click—missed opportunities.

Embrace God's grace, new mercies to start this day fresh, and strength to walk differently today.

"Let the past sleep, but let it sleep on the bosom of Christ, and go out into the irresistible future with Him" (Oswald Chambers).

REFLECT

1. Have you had a *real-life* encounter with injustice? If so, what?

2. What's the difference between poverty and justice?

3. What one new thing did you learn about the words "poverty" and "justice"?

4. How is Kingdom justice different than social justice?

5. Name some groups of people who need justice. You can refer to the table if you need to. Why is it sometimes hard to spot them? Do you have any connections to a specific group?

6. Contemplate how you would feel about that injustice happening to your parents, spouse, or children, and allow yourself silent reflection in order to feel the gravity of that situation.

7. Which of the five reasons to be personally involved connects with you?
   - I'll recognize Jesus.
   - Jesus will recognize me.
   - They belong to my family.
   - I'm one of the weak.
   - Limitless benefits.

8. Do you feel guilty or inadequate about past decisions? How can you "go out into the irresistible future with Him"?

2
LOVE THING

One can give without loving,
but one cannot love without giving.
—Amy Carmichael

Teaching is in my bloodline; I can't help it. It's genetically encrypted into my earliest memories of waiting for my father at school, playing in computer boxes, or being bored crazy as my parents annually raided local education stores. As a child I never understood why my parents put up with the long hours, stacks of papers, and small thanks. Now that I'm a teacher myself, I get it. It's the look in a student's eye when it finally sinks in, the success on the test after a long struggle, and most of all—the contagious love of learning.

That love isn't something that can be taught—it must be caught. During an internship I remember watching my supervising teacher introduce the theme of an upcoming musical. The musical's parade theme would involve balloons and floats and was going to be the greatest musical production ever. The teacher got the students to listen to the music and learn the song by selling the idea with skills rivaling a seasoned salesman.

This doesn't mean students always "feel" like learning. Even the best students convey a dislike for certain songs or subjects. Real love for learning is not just a warm, fuzzy feeling, but rather a passion to embrace challenges in order to build skills. Technical skills are the vehicle, but love's energy drives the engine.

In a book of techniques about helping those who are in need of justice, we must ask ourselves, *What's driving our engines?* Could what we call mercy really be self-determination, good works, or guilt? There's a vast desert of difference between duty, charity, pity, concern, kindness, and love.[1]

C. S. Lewis said, "There is a kindness in Love, but Love and Kindness are not coterminous, and when Kindness is separated from the other elements of Love, it involves a certain fundamental indifference to its object and even something like the contempt of it."[2]

Poor for Two Hours

One Thursday morning I was in a tired fog as I drove to the neighborhood grocery. As I got out of the car, I decided to put my gym bag in the trunk. Slamming the trunk door shut, I realized I was still holding my gym bag, but my purse was now locked in the trunk.

With my keys.

With my cell phone.

With my wallet.

No problem, I thought. *I'll just ask to use the phone at the grocery store customer service desk.* For some reason, though, the regular phone lines don't allow a call out of the building, so we had to track down a phone that would. The desk clerk was very patient, considering she had to babysit me while I called many friends and family. No one was answering. I felt terribly alone. I left a desperate message on my husband's cell phone.

His workplace was only a couple of miles away—close enough for me to walk there. Another desk clerk agreed to let me leave my gym bag. Then she looked at me and decided it was too cold for me to walk that far in my fleece. I told her I would be fine, but she offered her coat. I thought, *There's no way I'm taking her coat.* But she insisted, and I relented.

Self-consciousness rose into embarrassment as cars passed me while I walked on the long road inside a business office park. Did they wonder why I was walking down business streets? Did they think I was up to no good? Did they even notice me at all? Then I thought of the coat and was ashamed.

I advocate for children in Africa who are in need, but I don't notice people in need who are around me every day. I wonder why. When I go to a Compassion International event, I'm excited; the event is programmed and planned, and it captures my heart. But most of the time I'm not very engaged in the needs of others. In that moment, though, when I walked a couple of miles in a borrowed coat, it was as if God pulled the cover off a large black cesspool in my heart. The view of my heart from inside that coat wasn't pretty.

I would never have looked at a stranger and assessed that he or she needed a coat—*my* coat. I might have lent it to a friend if she had asked—a responsible friend who I was sure would return it. The desk clerk didn't seem concerned that I might forget to return her coat. In that one swift act she made me feel like an equal, preserving my dignity in the face of my humiliation. Both of the women I met that day went far beyond duty—or even mere concern. They showed me compassion, and it was jolting.

After my husband and I met up, he took me to unlock the trunk and retrieve my purse and keys. I returned the coat with my gratitude. All was fine. But as I finally checked out with my groceries, I heard another customer yelling at one of the ladies who had helped me. When I thought about how much junk customer service representatives put up with from the general public every day, I felt all the more humbled by the royal treatment they had showered on me.

It took that situation for me to begin to finally get it. Those ladies could have helped me without compassion. They could have allowed me to use the phone and store my things at the counter without extending such graciousness. They could have just done their jobs. Their heart attitudes could have been indifferent, passive, rude, mocking, or condescending.

It wasn't what they did as much as how they treated me.

Love: the Standard

Are our interactions, which may or may not involve money, rooted in duty, charity, pity, concern, kindness, or love? Are we advancing a cause or loving a human being? By what standard?

The definition of love can be found in 1 Corinthians 13:1-3:

If I speak in the tongues of men and of angels, but have not love, I am only a resounding gong or a clanging cymbal. If I have the gift of prophecy and can fathom all mysteries and all knowledge, and if I have a faith that can move mountains, but have not love, I am nothing. *If I give all I possess to the poor* and surrender my body to the flames, *but have not love, I gain nothing* (*emphasis added*).

So according to God's standard, aid is either given with love or given for no reason. Then God raises the bar even higher.

Love is patient, love is kind. It does not envy, it does not boast, it is not proud. It is not rude, it is not self-seeking, it is not easily angered, it keeps no record of wrongs. Love does not delight in evil but rejoices with the truth. It always protects, always trusts, always hopes, always perseveres (*1 Corinthians 13:4-7*).

I have broken trust with my loved ones through impatience, harshness, envy, rudeness, pride, selfishness, anger, and holding grudges. Love may never fail, but *I* have failed. I've fallen short in loving those who are easy to love, let alone those who challenge me.

After the initial humbling of those verses, there's a sweet relief about what love is not. I'm so glad that Paul did not write that love is waking up in the morning with a clear schedule, a song in my heart, and orchestral sounds descending from the sky. I'm glad he didn't say that love is being happy when my children disobey, my heart fluttering when my husband is grumpy, and looking forward to helping my neighbors find their lost dog—again.

No, love is not a romantic movie. Love is always a choice of will that impacts my feelings over time. I will fail, but I have a choice the next day to try again, to hope again, and to persevere.

Love: the Picture

But the standard isn't enough. The symbols aren't good enough—the pictures of God's love through friendship, marriage, and family have been twisted and corrupted. We need love itself—flesh to touch, words to hear. We need love with skin on, as Jesus Christ was when He lived among us. For the briefest time, through Him humans got to see, touch, and hear love.

How did Jesus say we should love? In John 15 He tells us that apart from Him we can do nothing. This is very similar to Paul's words when he said that giving without love is to gain nothing. A good deed that lowers the dignity of the recipient never leaves a lasting impact. Apart from Christ, apart from love, we can't help it. We steal the spotlight for someone else—ourselves.

Love: Dark and Light

Jesus had some things to say to those who did good works in order to glorify themselves. They were the Pharisees, or religious leaders of the day. To a Jew the Pharisees were the good people. Today we often say "Pharisee" to mean a hypocrite or a fake.

Be careful not to do your "acts of righteousness" before men, to be seen by them. If you do, you will have no reward from your Father in heaven. So when you give to the needy, do not announce it with trumpets, as the hypocrites do in the synagogues and on the streets, to be honored by men. I tell you the truth, they have received their reward in full. But when you give to the needy, do not let your left hand know what your right hand is doing, so that your giving may be in secret. Then your Father, who sees what is done in secret, will reward you *(Matthew 6:1-4).*

There is a deep darkness in getting the glory for ourselves. The poor become prey to our need to feel good about ourselves. In Mark Helprin's *Winter's Tale,* a doctor speaks of the ladies' aid society:

The great irony and perfect joke is that the wretches on the bottom of the barrel get these self-serving scum as champions! They feed off the poor—first materially, and then in spirit. . . . The ones who are always on your side, or so they think, are the ones who keep you down. Everything they do keeps you down. . . . Perfect! You can go on that way forever. What do they care? Excuse me: they do care. They want it that way.[3]

It's a gruesome picture of a parasite feeding on the weak. If our beneficiaries rise to independence, are we glad or worried about our own significance? Is it wrong to mention that we ourselves receive some good for helping the poor? Not at all if by that we mean that we're growing, changing, and healing, if we're removing layers of selfishness and finding a common brokenness with those we serve.

If we mean we're using the poor to feel good about ourselves, it's something different altogether. As the pendulum of popularity once again swings toward concerns about social justice, this must mean more than following the crowd. Could it be that it's all about us and not about them?

So it must be addressed. Why are we doing what we are doing? Is it really *love* if we're not giving all the glory to God? Could we be giving more anonymously? Are we willing to do it without notifying the local news and getting our name or business promoted? Are we striving to preserve the dignity of the recipient?

There is a balance. Even if we're discreet, some good deeds will inevitably be seen by others—the accountant who deducts our charitable contributions, those who partner with us in our charitable endeavors. What then?

You are the light of the world. A city on a hill cannot be hidden. Neither do people light a lamp and put it under a bowl. Instead they put it on its stand, and it gives light to everyone in the house. In the same way, let your light shine before men, that they may see your good deeds and praise your Father in heaven (*Matthew 5:14-16*).

When our hearts are right, and we're serving as an act of worship of Jesus Christ, our good deeds will direct praise back to God. This does not mean that we can wait until our motives are one-hundred-percent perfect. We try, we fail, we confess our mistakes, and then we serve again. We increase our dependence on Christ to help us do a better job the next time.

Love: the Sacrifice

So what does Jesus Christ have to do with generosity of spirit, sacrificial abandon, and caring for the poor? It's easy for us to think that we are rich, reaching down to help the poor. Jesus reveals that we are all poor and needy, and He's the one who reaches down to us. There is no "us" and "them."

We are all in need. We don't need another good example, pithy saying, or wise man. We need a heart transplant—new life that only God can give. We need Jesus, because He is God. He came to us even though He knew He would be misunderstood, rejected, beaten, and even killed. But He loved us and came anyway. He was raised from the dead to show us that the only way to new life is through Him.

We must not carry out any ministry without first understanding our deepest need—forgiveness for rebelling against Him. Have you come to Jesus? If not, would you start there today? Without Christ, we're hypocrites giving physical riches to try to make up for the spiritual riches we lack in ourselves. Do you have more unanswered questions about a relationship with Jesus? Call 888-NEED-HIM, or visit <www.needhim.org>.

For those of us who know Him, does His love for us impact how we treat others? How much do we really love Christ? Do we love the things of Christ? Do we love what He loves? We must be doggedly committed to interaction with the poor by following Jesus' model: perseverance when close friends and family don't understand why or what we're doing, servanthood in a climate of rejection or apathy, commitment to no longer consider the weak as a "pet project" for our own political, spiritual, or social leverage. We can care for those who will never offer a kind smile and a thankful word in return, because this is what Christ did.

Beautiful Interruptions—Dana's Story

As I was driving today, I passed a homeless man and was reminded of something that happened last summer when my husband and I were in Colombia. After a long day of mission work, we cleaned up and went across the street for ice cream.

A young woman and a little boy around six years old stood begging for money. We noticed them, gave a few coins, and got in line for ice cream. We were feeling pretty pleased with ourselves until we saw another couple on our team.

Justin and Angie asked the young woman her name and invited her and the little boy to join them for ice cream. Wow! Why didn't we think of that? They took the time to get to know the young woman, introduce her to their friends, and spend the evening together. They showed her that she was loved and valued. They even invited her back later in the week to pick up some groceries. It was truly a modern day story of the Good Samaritan. God used it as a humbling experience and a reminder for us not to pass by those we meet in our everyday lives.

Overseas or in America, real mercy requires my willingness to let go of my agenda. Last spring I found myself working on a yard project when a neighbor showed up. Honestly, I hate it when that happens. I don't like to be interrupted. I want to finish a project to completion. At that moment, I could have chosen to continue my project and blow her off or stop to really listen to find out what was going on in her life. Though it's not always the case, thankfully that time I stopped and listened, and she shared her health concerns with me.

I'm learning to see people as Jesus sees them and love them as He would love them—being His physical hands and feet. It's hard to fathom what loving and caring "for the least of these" really looks like. Am I really portraying God's love accurately to the world around me?

Love in Real Life

We know we should help. So what holds us back? What keeps us from loving well as we serve? What stops us from joining in to help? Maybe these are just a few of the things that prevent action on our part:

- Unsteady emotions
- Discomfort
- Lack of direction
- Lifestyle change

It's Okay to Feel

Learning to feel carries with it both a blessing and a curse: a blessing because those feelings are what lead us out of ourselves; a curse because once out we can never again go back and enjoy the simple pleasures of a self-absorbed life. For suffering sensitizes us not only to the world around us, which is needy, but to the world within us, which is needier still, and ultimately to the world beyond us, which we long for in so many ways (Ken Gire).[4]

We all have our hangups that keep us from loving the way we should. Mine are emotional. Please don't ask me to feel something. Your pain threatens to engulf me, washing away the sand of my facade until broken places are exposed like brittle shells upon the surf—broken pieces of judgment, self-righteousness, weaknesses, sorrow, and failure.

The curse—the exposure of my soul's wrecked beachfront property—what an eyesore! The blessing—the exposure of my soul's wrecked beachfront property—restoration is on the way.

Time alone with Christ becomes necessary renovation, not a luxury item. Unless I'm consistently being real with Jesus about my sin and my selfishness to empty myself out before Him, I cannot trust my emotions around anyone else. I can expose brokenness to you, because I don't need your approval or reciprocation. My identity is secure. I can give my most precious commodity—letting you in.

In a beautiful twist of nature, I don't drown. The more I am concerned with the pain of another, the more my pain diminishes in size and is healed.

It's Okay to Be Uncomfortable

The biggest obstacle to loving the broken is fear—fear of the unknown, safety concerns, social issues, lack of time and resources. All are real. It's scary to think about putting ourselves in an unknown situation with unknown people. The next chapter is designed to help overcome those fears. We often dread fear, because we long for what is comfortable. Is the purpose a comfortable life? No, it's a joy-filled, abundant life.

It occurs to me that there have probably been many times I have traded real joy for comfort. The discomfort that comes from loving those who are not particularly lovable comes from feeling exposed because we don't really know what to expect. God will cover that exposure. In Isaiah 58:8 God says that He is our "rear guard." In battle, the soldier is most vulnerable if attacked from behind—where he can't see what's coming at him. The Lord promises us that when we help the poor, He has our backs—He will be our rear guard.

It's Okay to Have Questions

Kingdom justice requires more of us and less of our big ideas. Don't underestimate the power of simply treating others well. Start with treating others as equals; listen, and encourage them. Work with them as a teammate when aid is offered.[5]

There are no simple or easy answers anyway. It takes partnerships and resources and working together with others who have experience in aiding the poor. There's no need to try to figure everything out on our own and waste time reinventing the wheel. (See the Appendix for lists of resources.)

It's Okay to Live Upside Down

"You know the grace of our Lord Jesus Christ, that though he was rich, yet for your sakes he became poor, so that you through his poverty might become rich" (2 Corinthians 8:9).

You may have been led to believe that allying yourself with someone who can't pay you back drains your time and resources and won't advance your career, that it's smart business practice to be endorsed by someone with a big name and to market those credentials. It takes a conscious shift from that mind-set to live a different lifestyle.

Love cost Christ everything, but it's through Christ's poverty we became rich. It's by living out that extravagant love example that we find the richest life imaginable. We settle for meager comforts when He wants to give us keys to the palace.

But it's a palace I can't see or touch and comforts I can't feel. There's pain in the death of selfishness—a struggle battling for my time, my will, my emotions. But right past the pain is life—real life, upside down.

It's Okay to Long for Restoration

We're captivated by beauty. We shop for stylish clothes, elegant homes, and top-quality products. We're drawn to a restored painting, a piece of great music, or an engaging personality. Souls long for the beautiful restoration of what's broken. We're inversely repelled by tragedy, sorrow, and pain. But there's a beauty far greater than the outside trappings of clothing or hairstyle. Beauty resides in humility, mercy, and tenderness. I often have found the bleak material world of what seems broken a perfect canvas for the vivid contrast of the beauty of restoration.

A brightness exists that can be seen only by moving out of a dark tunnel.

A sweetness that can be heard only after a long silence.

A warmth that can be felt only after a long chill.

A resurrection of spring that can be found only after a long winter.

Where there are prophecies, they will cease; where there are tongues, they will be stilled; where there is knowledge, it will pass away. For we know in part and we prophesy in part, *but when perfection comes, the imperfect disappears.* . . . Now we see but a poor reflection as in a mirror; then we shall see face to face. Now I know in part; then I shall know fully, even as I am fully known. And now these three remain: faith, hope and love. But the greatest of these is love (*1 Corinthians 13:8-13, emphasis added*).

REFLECT

1. How do you choose to move in love's direction when you don't feel like it?

2. What's the difference between serving with duty and serving with charity, pity, concern, kindness, or love? How can you grow in this area?

3. How can love become dark?

4. Do you accept Jesus' sacrifice of love for you? If your answer is yes, how are you plugging into Christ for your motivation and energy to serve the poor?

5. In real life, we face obstacles to love. Which one of the following is the hardest to conquer?
   Basic fear
   Unsteady emotions
   Discomfort
   Lack of direction
   Lifestyle change

3
DAILY BREAD

Sometimes you have to jump off cliffs and
grow wings on the way down.
—Ray Bradbury

I'm having one of those days. My husband's car stopped half-way between our house and the repair shop. We're now waiting on a tow truck—in the dark in the right-turn lane. The car's emergency flashers pulse a signal in my brain: SOS—SOS—SOS. *God, do you see this? Do you see me?*

My mind jumps to other events of the day: cavities to be filled. SOS—SOS—SOS. A student laments, "I hate this!" SOS—SOS—SOS. Health problems—again. SOS—SOS—SOS. Financial strain in my weary husband's face. SOS—SOS—SOS.

Daily bread.

It's so hard to trust God's hand to take care of me— the hand I cannot see.

Some people have a "happy place" they go to. I went to my crazy place. I'm not proud of it. I screamed at my husband and started to cry. It wasn't his fault—he was doing his best. It wasn't my fault either. It wasn't even about the car. Please, not one more thing tonight. Finally the yellow glow of the tow truck flashers arrive, finally the repair shop, then finally home.

The next morning I cried out to God in a way I hadn't in years. The car breaking down was the last straw. The weariness of holding it all together for the past few months had caught up with me.

What did Jesus really mean? Would He give me my daily bread as promised? That seemed unfathomable, when I know the hard reality that today 30,000 children will die from preventable causes.[1] What happens to their sustenance for the day? If we don't all receive our daily portion, why are we supposed to ask?

That morning my daily reading was in the gospel of Luke. Jesus was telling the disciples not to worry about what they would eat, drink or wear. He feeds the birds—how much more surely will He feed us? He makes the flowers beautiful—how much more certainly will He give us what we need? Where is my faith?

Then the beautiful, almost forgotten part at the end: "Do not be afraid, little flock, for your Father has been pleased to give you the kingdom" (Luke 12:32).

Once again I started to cry. I was that little one in the flock. I knew I wasn't supposed to worry, but everyone worries—why was it such a big deal?

My fear eclipsed the goodness of God. My good Father sees me here and sees that I'm afraid. I want little things, and He's ready to give me life in the Kingdom. He is my provision. He is my daily bread.

Most important, there's a sweet provision in times when things are withheld from me. *No bread today?* Lessons in hungering after Him.[2] *No friends to comfort me?* Lessons in the unfailing love from Christ. *No healing?* Lessons in longing for permanent restoration.

That was a turning point in my life. When I hold back on giving, it's not a matter of not knowing I *should* give. We all know that, right? The obstacle is not intellectual—it's emotional.

I finally had to admit that I was afraid. I guess I didn't want to own that. I thought other people had problems with giving, but me? I do my part! I'm an advocate for a major charitable organization.

But God was saying, "No, Amber—you have a problem of your own," one common to the human condition. And He had spent months trying to get my attention.

Something would break—the water heater for instance, and I would hold back on giving a gift or my time or financial support for someone going on a mission trip. Then a health insurance bill would arrive: *I guess I'll have to work extra hours.*

I was in a cycle of self-protection, and I didn't even see it. I wanted complete control, every dollar stacking up and making sense. I doubted that God would provide no matter what.

I wish I could say it was a past problem, but I battle it every day of my life. I want to do what I can on my own and not have to rely on God. My emotions are deeply linked to my physical condition. I feel my fear as deeply as I would feel a broken bone. Sometimes I would prefer physical injury to this fear. It shakes me to the core to feel weak and dependent.

A few years ago I would have blamed my circumstances as the instigators of my fear. I know better now. My fear is quantified in inverse proportion to my faith—an indicator as precise as a thermometer of my inward spiritual condition.

Does it really work? When bills, family, and crisis situations shake us down until nothing's left, will we choose fear or generosity? We're called to give upside down as we have opportunity—sacrificially, generously, and joyfully.

This is easy to say but difficult to grasp. What does this upside-down giving look like? The following stories of real women are real pictures with living scriptures as the picture frame. It intrigues me that these women, despite their deep need for provision in their own lives, moved past fear to vibrant generosity.

Give Upside Down

"God is able to make all grace abound to you, so that in all things at all times, having all that you need, you will abound in every good work" (2 Corinthians 9:8).

Got Cereal? Andi's Story of Financial Provision

My husband, Jack, and I grew up in the Midwest and got married in our early twenties. We had great jobs, and financial problems weren't even a distant thought. After we started having children, our income was cut in half when I became a stay-at-home mom.

Right after our second child was born, Jack was offered a job at church. We both prayed about it and felt God confirm in our hearts that he should accept it. It was really scary that our only source of income was about to be cut again.

About a year later, after our third child was born, our financial situation reached a crisis. We had put the kids to bed and were sitting on the couch, just looking at each other. We normally have a bedtime snack, but even that had been cut. Three meals a day was sufficient, but I wasn't totally being filled. We weren't going hungry or coming close to what people in other countries go through, but it wore on us.

The next Sunday morning I was walking down the hall at church to drop the kids off in the nursery. A friend of mine stopped me and said, "Andi, I don't need this box of baby cereal. Do you want it?"

I was just starting my youngest daughter, Jenna, on that same cereal. I started to cry. God showed himself to me in that little box of cereal and reminded me that if we seek first His kingdom, everything else will be given to us as well. God's provision is right on time.

The God who is big enough to create the vast Milky Way is also small enough and personal enough to provide me with a two-dollar box of cereal and the comfort and peace of mind that He's here with me. He cares for my every need.

Life hasn't slowed down at all. I'm now blessed with five children under the age of seven. As our family has increased, so have the stories of provision—from revamping our finances to a salary increase for my husband to the love and care poured out from our church family each time a new baby is born. God goes far past provision to abundant blessings. In the last three years we've been provided free vacations!

Our ability to trust God with finances has impacted our children as well. Recently after some neighbors lost their home in a fire, Jillian, our second child, emptied her savings to contribute to that family's need. Seeing and helping us organize a neighborhood relief fund, our kids know giving is a way of life. We can be that right-on-time provision for someone else.

Giving is upside down when everything inside us screams, "Take what you need now! Give the leftovers!" God's call is different. Jack and Andi took a huge risk. He felt called to work at church, and she felt called to work at home. They both felt called to keep giving to others outside their own family. They gave first and then watched God provide.

GIVE AS YOU HAVE OPPORTUNITY

"As we have opportunity, let us do good to all people, especially to those who belong to the family of believers" (Galatians 6:10).

Ka-chow! Kelly's Story of Emotional Provision

A few weeks ago I had a particularly weepy evening, and the Lord showed His love to me through my sweet little Jensen.

We were all in bed when around 3 AM I heard Jensen crying. I got up and brought him to bed with me. He quickly fell asleep, but I was awake and couldn't stop thinking about Erik.

I rolled over and started looking at the collage of pictures on the wall. I started sobbing. All of a sudden I felt this little pat on my shoulder. It was Jensen, still sleeping but reaching out and comforting me. It was so precious, and it was as if the Lord himself said, "It's okay. I'm here. I'm with you."

After a few pats, Jensen said, "Ka-chow!" Then he rolled over and started snoring. I laughed so hard. If you've ever seen a certain animated film, you know what I'm talking about. Jensen walks around saying, "Ka-chow!" all the time.

It definitely brought me out of my down mood. God's grace and love, through my children, reminded me of His care.

Kelly became a young widow caring for her two little boys after her husband passed away with cancer. Erik and Kelly were devoted to college ministry. Kelly is still involved with Campus Crusade for Christ, an organization focused on turning lost students into

Christ-centered laborers. She also takes opportunities to serve by speaking and writing about this difficult chapter in her life.

I've often seen young college girls' faces light up when they see Kelly. She's quietly ministering to our local community of believers by discipling these young women. No one would have faulted her if she had retreated from service to tend only to her family's needs. But she's taking this difficult opportunity to be an encouragement to all who know her.

GIVE SACRIFICIALLY

"King David replied to Araunah, 'No, I insist on paying the full price. I will not take for the LORD what is yours, or sacrifice a burnt offering that costs me nothing'" (1 Chronicles 21:24).

Home Front—Sheri's Story of Physical Provision

I used to think that if I made the right decisions, I could keep life running smoothly. However, the military lifestyle creates a somewhat unpredictable life. After John and I married, the frequent relocations began to unravel my designs for stability.

Then came even bigger tests—stressful pregnancies, evacuation during Hurricane Ivan, and fear about John's safety during training.

While John studied and perfected drills, I was finishing my own personal basic training. The Lord was preparing me to trust Him with something bigger.

The day John deployed to Iraq, we kissed good-bye through our tears. There was little time to give in to my emotions—I needed to focus on getting the boys home and keeping them calm.

Just a few days later, I received a phone call that my grandfather had passed away. I flew across the country, alone with my two small children. It was a difficult flight, to say the least. The kids screamed most of the time, we endured long layovers, and the airline lost one of the kids' car seats. My emotions were raw, and I was not even at the funeral yet.

After the funeral dinner, Andrew, my two-year old, became extremely ill. We finally realized that he had gotten into some rat poison at a relative's home. I rushed him to the hospital, and he had blood drawn. The worst part was waiting several days to know what damage had been done. The worst-case scenario was the possibility of massive internal bleeding.

The boys and I returned home not knowing what the final outcome would be for Andrew. Weeks later he was tested again, and those tests showed that he was going to be fine. I realized right then that I really had no control over my life. God had kept my little boy completely safe; the boys and I would rely on Him for physical protection. When craziness did happen, He would have to help us find the best course of action.

I relied on God every day during the next months. We faced health scares—scarlet fever and strep—I locked myself out on our second-story balcony while the kids were inside the house running wild, and the security system sounded a false alarm in the middle of the night. I had no choice but to learn to stay calm. Again and again, God gave me the mental clarity to make the next decision. Most important of all, I trusted God for my husband's safety.

I can look back on all that now, and I'm thankful for the difficulties. When my husband was deployed for the second time—an even more dangerous deployment—it was easier to handle. John is doing exactly what God wants him to do, and my calm spirit lets him be completely focused on his job.

Difficulties still come, but I no longer react with panic. God's perfect love for us is sufficient to carry us through hard times.

Sheri has lived through pressure that most of us don't face. She could have given in to the panic, shut down, and stopped giving. She not only cares for her husband and young boys but also gives support to other women. She's writing children's books to help kids whose parents are in military service.

GIVE GENEROUSLY

"Give generously to him and do so without a grudging heart; then because of this the LORD your God will bless you in all your work and in everything you put your hand to" (Deuteronomy 15:10).

Mother Teresa's Story of Spiritual Provision

Some time ago a man came to our home saying, "Mother, there is a family with eight children who have not eaten for a long time. You've got to do something." So I took the rice and went. When I arrived, I could see the hunger shining from their eyes. I gave the rice to the mother, she took it, divided it in two, and went out. When she returned, I asked her, "Where did you go?"

She said, pointing to her neighbor's home, "They are hungry also."[3]

This story still takes my breath away. My inclination is to give after I'm sure I have enough. I'm not sure I even know what "enough" really is. It's fitting that the story I found of the woman who gave generously was actually poor herself. She isn't named, but her story is linked with Mother Teresa forever. I don't know how to give like that.

If we believe this story is about the gift of rice from Mother Teresa, we miss the entire story. This unnamed woman made a hard choice in that moment, and God provided the spiritual life strong and deep enough to overflow in kindness to those around her.

GIVE JOYFULLY

"Out of the most severe trial, their overflowing joy and their extreme poverty welled up in rich generosity" (2 Corinthians 8:2).

Jesus, the Ultimate Provision

Some time after this, Jesus crossed to the far shore of the Sea of Galilee (that is, the Sea of Tiberias), and a great crowd of people followed him because they saw the miraculous signs he had performed on the sick. Then Jesus went up on a mountainside and sat down with his disciples. The Jewish Passover Feast was near.

When Jesus looked up and saw a great crowd coming toward him, he said to Philip, "Where shall we buy bread for these people to eat?" He asked this only to test him, for he already had in mind what he was going to do.

Philip answered him, "Eight months' wages would not buy enough bread for each one to have a bite!"

Another of his disciples, Andrew, Simon Peter's brother, spoke up, "Here is a boy with five small barley loaves and two small fish, but how far will they go among so many?"

Jesus said, "Have the people sit down." There was plenty of grass in that place, and the men sat down, about five thousand of them. Jesus then took the loaves, gave thanks, and distributed to those who were seated as much as they wanted. He did the same with the fish.

When they had all had enough to eat, he said to his disciples, "Gather the pieces that are left over. Let nothing be wasted." So they gathered them and filled twelve baskets with the pieces of the five barley loaves left over by those who had eaten.

After the people saw the miraculous sign that Jesus did, they began to say, "Surely this is the Prophet who is to come into the world." Jesus, knowing that they intended to come and make him king by force, withdrew again to a mountain by himself (*John 6:1-15*).

Jesus is faced with a dilemma. He's exhausted and faced with a crowd of hungry people. The disciples have no food, and the crowd's spiritual hunger is greater than their physical hunger.

Our dilemma may be similar. Exhaustion, physical and spiritual needs surround us, and our resources are limited. Does the little we have to offer even make a difference? As Philip calculates what this would cost and Andrew searches for food, we find a child willing to offer the little he has. We know this boy is poor, because his meal is barley bread and fish.[4] Would he be willing to go hungry in order to share?

I relate to the disciples more than to the little boy. Often I calculate why I don't have sufficient funds to give, or I find small provisions and doubt how useful they will be. What can be accomplished with the broken pieces of my hurts, my small financial contributions, my imperfect skills, my weak stamina?

GIVE THE LITTLE YOU HAVE

Nothing we give is wasted, even when we aren't sure if it's good enough.

I struck up a special bond with a teenager named Shawna one summer during a mentorship program. We sat next to each other on outings, shared snacks, and laughed and talked together. She came from a family of seven and was often the caretaker while her mother worked. At summer's end I took Shawna and her friend shopping for glass jars. As we walked past the infant department, they wanted to stop to admire the baby clothes, saying they wanted a baby. And they meant soon! This obsession grew from their connections with older sisters and cousins who were already teen moms.

I talked with them about a vision for their lives and their spouses. I reminded them of what the Bible says about purity and asked them what they wanted for their futures. They wrote down their "wish lists" for their futures on pretty stationery, along with a commitment to abstinence, and sealed their lists in those glass jars.

I returned home at the end of the summer and lost that daily contact with Shawna. I ended up writing many letters to her that went unanswered, and I was unsure if anything of substance had been accomplished during our summer together.

A few months later, a teacher from the mentorship program mailed me a copy of one of Shawna's journal entries. The kids had been given an assignment to write about their best friend. Shawna had listed me, "Miss Amber," as her best friend. She recounted the day we filled the glass jars, as well as some fun times we had. I was floored that she remembered me and that day. I was blessed to realize that the time we spent together had had a greater impact than I thought. What I did was so little, but God had multiplied the results.

That same summer I met another student in the program named K. J. He was rowdy, disobedient, and violent. He was one of those kids who had me praying for patience as soon as I met him. He was disrespectful to staff and did his best to interrupt group activities. We loved him anyway. The male staffers played basketball with him and encouraged him to be a leader with the younger kids. When we summer interns left, we assumed we had made no difference in K. J.'s life. We later learned that he had changed.

Devastated after the shooting of his sister, he accepted Christ and made decisions to separate his behaviors from those of his violent surroundings. He bragged to a teacher that a classmate flipped him off, and he wanted to hit him. "It's a good thing Jesus is in my heart, because I just walked away."

What kind fellow workers, to give us the good news about the results of our labors! In real life we don't always get updates on the impact we have in others' lives, and the things we do may not have any impact for years. I always want to see immediate results to keep my motivation up. It's hard to want to keep giving when there are no visible results or instantly changed lives.

Just like that little boy in the Bible story, I must offer Christ my "loaves and fish" with no expectations and no demands. The God who created the universe can surely stretch the dollars, multiply the results, and change lives. What a privilege!

I don't have to give. That little boy was presenting bread to the Bread of Life. He gave food to the one who controls all resources in the world. That little boy was a participant in the only miracle recorded in every gospel account. Can you imagine the moment when he realized what Christ did with the little he gave? It was hysterical joy that eclipsed any fear, any sacrifice, any pain of loss.

"Just as the loaves increased when they were broken, the Lord has granted those things necessary to the beginning of this work, and when they (are) given out, they will be multiplied by His inspiration, so that in this task of mine I shall not only suffer no poverty of ideas but shall rejoice in wonderful abundance" (Augustine).

The courageous stories of others inspire me to walk through my fear so that I can
- give upside down,
- give as I have opportunity,
- give sacrificially,
- give generously,
- give joyfully,
- give what little I have.

Daily Bread

A year and a half after my "SOS" when our car broke down, I still fear deeply, reverberating from my best friend's home foreclosure to my own checkbook as we wade through the deep waters of my husband's job loss. I'm relearning a valuable lesson. *What am I really hungry for?*

I have enough to eat every day, but I'm still afraid of not having enough. I must face the fact that I don't really want daily bread. What I want is a guarantee that my bills will be paid till the end of my days. I want to possess the emotional, mental, and spiritual resources to handle everything perfectly. I want "enough," but what I *need* is God.

Daily bread. I'm empty, but security will not fill me.

Daily bread—not what He *gives,* but *Him.*

REFLECT

1. Have you ever had a time, like the little boy who gave the loaves to Jesus, when you gave past your fears? Why did you decide to give? How did you feel afterward?

2. Can you think of a time that, because of your fear, you didn't give? What were you afraid of losing if you gave? The money for your family responsibilities? The time you need for other tasks? Power and status? Other?

3. How has God provided for you financially, emotionally, physically, spiritually, in the past?

4. From the list of types of giving that follows, which is your strength? Which is your weakness?
   • Giving upside down
   • Giving as you have opportunity
   • Giving sacrificially
   • Giving generously
   • Giving joyfully
   • Giving what little you have

5. What *one* thing can you do to improve your giving?

4

At Home

We think that poverty is only being hungry, naked, and homeless.
The poverty of being unwanted, unloved, and uncared for
is the greatest poverty. We must start in our own homes
to remedy this kind of poverty.

—Mother Teresa

July 1984 blazes a record-setting heat wave. I scoot my seven-year-old backside across searing hot vinyl seats to the far side of the tiny Chevette. My little sister starts whining about who will get the "cool" side, sending my mom's internal temperature way past one hundred degrees. The chorus of "Mom!" sets off her crazy mode before the car even leaves the driveway.

We drive to my dad's work—his chauffeurs for the day, adrift in our little island inferno. Every minute is an eternity when you're seven. My extrovert sister wants to play. My introvert self wants her to shut up. Her toy scuttles across the sacred center line of personal space, and I throw it back to her side. She screams.

"Wait until your father . . ." reaches our ears from the front seat. Silence. Dark clouds descend on our minds.

My thoughts whip with the wind against the flagpole. *I hate my life! Other kids aren't stuck in a car. Other kids don't have an annoying sister. Other kids have air conditioning at home. Mom doesn't understand. I have it the worst of any possible kid anywhere, any time, ever. I hate my life!*

Once we're back home, my anger continues to pulse with each clank of silverware as I set the table for our meal. The sunlight flashes off the refrigerator door. The white background contrasts with the black-faced little girl's photo. *I hate my life! Other kids aren't stuck in a car. Other kids don't have an annoying sister. Other kids have air conditioning at home. Nobody understands. I have it the worst of any possible kid anywhere, any time, ever. I—*

I stop and stare at that photo.

I have it the worst?

Of any kid?

Ever?

The little girl has dirty clothes. I have lots of dresses for church.

She's barefoot. I have many shoes.

It looks really hot there—much worse than here.

Her brother died. My sister isn't really that bad.

The little girl needs our help just to live.

Shock and relief broke into my little world that day. It was the first time I remember feeling empathy for someone else.

I saw the little Kenyan girl's face daily, the lone portrait on a snowy canvas. Mom said I wrote letters and read letters—I really don't remember. My childhood memories grow fainter with the passing of time. But I remember the photo. I don't know her name, but something deep, strong, and important was etched on my young life by her photo. Poverty was real. Poverty had a face. Poverty had a name.

Most importantly, poverty had hope.

My family had no money for extras. So if we, who scraped by, helped support a child every month, it must have been important. Out of my family's desperate situation came the most important contribution to my young life—the gift of clarity. I began that day to see past my own needs to the needs of others.

"Each of you should look not only to your interests but to the interests of others" (Philippians 2:4).

One person made a difference. My stay-at-home mom with no car of her own brushed our hair, read to us, and sang songs with us. She lived justice and mercy without one phone call to Washington, without joining one committee, and without leaving her house. One person changed two lives—the little girl in the photo and the little girl in her home. Those childhood memories evolved into adolescent emotions that crystallized into adult convictions to help the poor.

As an adult, I advocate for Compassion International, the same organization my parents supported financially so many years ago.

You may be wondering what you can do and thinking that you have no idea where to start. You may be wondering where you fit into Kingdom justice.

SOMETHING FOR EVERYONE

It might be easier to write, "God wants you to _____." But that would cheat you out of a remarkable journey. Don't get hung up on the unknown destination. Let's start with where you are right now.

What's your life look like today? Are you young and longing to be taken seriously? Are you single? Are you in a busy career? Are you raising kids? Are you caring for an aging parent? Are you sick? Are you retired?

What's your schedule look like? All women have life stuff. We shop, cook, clean, pay bills, check e-mail, plan holidays, buy clothes, do hobbies, plan home projects, and keep up with family and friends. Let's start with those things we do already. What if it were really possible to make a difference as you do in everyday life?

What you do in your everyday life is who you really are.

It's possible to create the life you want working within your life stage and your unique schedule. The trick is not to look at your sister, neighbor, or friend and try to do what she's doing. Your story is unique, and only you can tell it. No one else is quite like you!

No master chef cooks with every ingredient in the kitchen. She finds what works with her talents and will suit the needs of those whom she's serving.

Will you walk with me into our very own fully-stocked gourmet kitchen? We can peruse the shelves of "lists" as a cook would survey her ingredients. We aren't going to try everything at once. We're going to find *one thing* that seems fun and go with it. Can you think of a better idea that fits your schedule? Can you take an idea listed and change it? You can make the recipe your own.

In the next section you'll find practical ways to help the needy without leaving your front door. After wading through much research with long explanations—and a big headache—I keep descriptions here short and sweet. Happy helping!

COMPUTER

GoodSearch. This site is my home page and search engine. GoodSearch will donate one cent to the charity organization of your choice each time you search. More than 55,000 organizations are already registered. If yours isn't on the site, you can register it in a few seconds. Donations add up fast. One nonprofit has earned more than $12,000.

Be sure to also check out the GoodShop tool. Start from this site when you shop brand names like Amazon, Best Buy, and Travelocity, and a percentage of your purchase will be donated to charity. Online shopping has the bonus of comparing prices, saving time, and saving gas money.
<www.goodsearch.com>

The Hunger Site. This site features awareness of hunger, child health, breast cancer, literacy, the rainforest, and animal rescue. Each click results in a donation to that cause. You can also purchase items from the online store.
<www.thehungersite.com>

Ripple. This site funds clean water, food, and education with your daily clicks. Ripple also features a search engine. To add to the giving power, you can link the Ripple "give" button directly to your Web site, blog, or social networking page.
<www.ripple.org>

Free Rice. What a fun brain break! For me a simple game of computer solitaire helps de-clutter my thoughts. Try this fun new vocabulary game in which every correct answer you choose pro-

vides a donation of twenty grains of rice to an impoverished country. Give somebody around the world a break while you take yours.
<www.freerice.com>

Free Poverty. Okay, I wasn't so good at this one. I did much better on the vocabulary game, but this fun site improved my geography skills. Locate cities and landmarks on a map, and the site donates ten cups of water to a poor country. I liked the feature that still added cups if the guess was close but not exact.
<www.freepoverty.com>.

Desktop Picture. Use the power of advertising to your advantage. What motivates you to keep on track to help others? I now have a landscaped picture of the hometown of my favorite author, George MacDonald. Seeing what inspired him to write helps me keep going on the days that I don't feel like it. What inspires you? Nature, music, art, or a picture of someone in poverty?

Subscription List. Activism ideas delivered to your inbox. Wouldn't it be nice if someone from your favorite nonprofit did all the legwork and delivered updates to you personally? This is already a reality for most nonprofits. The action steps vary from letters written, prayer requests, or just updates. Just click on your charity's Web site to see what it offers.

Social Networking, Blogs, and Web Sites. Add a charity's banner or link to your page. "Become a fan," or "invite a friend" to join your cause.

Prisoner Released! I couldn't believe it when I saw the update. A pastor was released from prison! The prisoner's government bowed to the pressure of piles of letters from around the world. When I decided to write my letter, I found I could choose from encouraging phrases and Bible verses. It was then translated into another language. I printed and mailed the letter. The prisoner for the gospel halfway around the world received it and was encouraged. Sometimes I can even e-mail the foreign officials directly. Be sure to follow each specific site's guidelines. For general help, see the letter-writing suggestions in the Appendix.

HOUSEWORK

Donate Business Attire. Help give local disadvantaged women the needed professional look for job interviews and job success. This organization also helps mentor these women after they secure a job. <www.dressforsuccess.org>.

Donate Cell Phones. You can help the victims of domestic violence, AIDS, world hunger, soldiers overseas, or even set up a phone drive to help your charity. Be sure to erase any phone lists or other stored information to reduce identity theft. Some of the sites have a cell phone data eraser. Look for the pink eraser icon.

<www.phones4charity.org>

<www.recellular.com>

<www.cellphonesforsoldiers.com>

Donate Computers. Outdated equipment can be refurbished for schools and nonprofits. Some areas in the country even arrange pickup from your house.

<www.pcsforschools.org>

Donate Rewards. Do you get rewards back from your debit or credit card? Studies have shown that most people do not keep track of those rewards. Most reward sites will allow donations to sick children and parents, military spouses, and others. Visit the Web site of your credit card or airline to learn more.

Garage Sale. Involve your family in a "clean sweep." Set the timer some Saturday afternoon to see who can come up with the most unused items in the least amount of time. Then sell those items in a garage sale. Donate proceeds to your charity. Multi-house garage sales also work if you're raising funds for adoption or mission trips. Don't forget to plan to give unsold items to a single mom, a family in need, or arrange for a charity such as the Salvation Army to pick them up.

Online Sales. Too busy for a garage sale? Sell unwanted items on eBay. By registering with MissionFish, you can select a percentage of your sale to go to the charity of your choice. The listing appears with a special ribbon to let buyers know that a percentage is going to charity.

Zwaggle, a swapping site for kids' items, allows the points you accrue to be donated to charity. Donated points earn a tax write-off.

<www.zwaggle.com>

Home Maintenance. Dreary tasks such as shoveling snow, painting, or mowing the lawn become meaningful and fun if you not only do your own but also have your family donate its time to help a neighbor in need. Could those tasks grow into a small side-business for your older child or your family? Give coupon discounts to seniors, veterans, or the disabled.

Really Clean. So what does cleaning have to do with kingdom justice or poverty? The most impoverished parts of the world have often been dumping grounds for toxic waste. Many of the working poor have the highest exposure to toxins at work.[1]

Toxins come from pesticides, prescription medicines, fertilizers, or cleaners. Buy safer cleaners and don't flush unsafe substances, such as medicine. Read labels carefully. Some products mislead with "eco-images" and "natural" labeling. Be careful to understand fact versus fiction regarding the environmental movement.[2] Do you want more information? The Cornwall Alliance champions stewardship care with biblical balance.

<www.cornwallalliance.org>

Do you want to see what's really in your products? Use Good-Guide to gauge the safety of what you are using in your home. For real economic savings and peace of mind, consumers can make their own cleaners. The best way to know what's in your products is to put the ingredients in yourself.[3]

<www.goodguide.com>

Cooking

- For the sick
- For someone with a new baby
- For someone who has adopted a baby
- For a single parent
- For a visitation/funeral meal

- For a family living with a long-term illness or disability
- For someone who has lost a job

Sell Your Cooking Project

- Family cookbook
- Lemonade/cookie stand
- Homemade items in a farmers' market
- Pitch-in dinner at which the money normally spent eating out is donated

<www.washingtonwomenade.org>

HOBBIES

Gardening. In 2004 about thirty-five million Americans went hungry. That's a surprising four out of ten Americans between the ages of twenty and sixty-five.[4] With rising grocery costs, food banks value fresh produce that adds key nutrition to diets. In 2005 Plant a Row for the Hungry distributed ten million pounds of produce in the United States and Canada. Planting an extra row of produce in your garden can make a real difference.

<www.gardenwriters.org>

Reading. Sell your unwanted books to BetterWorld, and get paid on the spot. You can also buy books (similar to Amazon) with free postage in the United States. This helps save books from landfills, and the profits help fund global literacy. Libraries can donate books as well.

<www.betterworldbooks.com>

Knitting Groups. Many churches create knitting groups. This is one activity that draws women of all ages. The groups knit blankets, scarves, and hats for women's shelters or baby clothes and blankets for the local crisis pregnancy center. Organizations request that you contact them first before knitting to find out what they need. Make sure the yarn is new and the items you donate are clean. Find free knitting tips and patterns online. Warm Woolies even offers free yarn for those who regularly knit for them.

<www.warmwoolies.org>
<www.projectlinus.org>

Knit-Wits—Jessica's Story

My coworker is a skilled knitter. She mentioned to me that she always thought about knitting baby items. I jumped in and said, "Let's do it!" As someone who had never knit, I didn't know what I was getting myself into. It was a comedy from the time the eight of us started learning to the oddly shaped projects we turned out. We rightly named ourselves the "knit-wits." My coworker's skills were advanced, and she can make beautiful hats and scarves; but we decided that with our skills we would just do colored squares and she would put them together into quilt patterns. She was so patient in teaching us and working with our mistakes.

An extra bonus was to learn that our company will support the efforts of employees who do volunteer work. For us, that meant that the company furnished our yarn and needles.

Our first quilt went to a homeless shelter. The next piece will go to a neonatal unit. Because I'm in the healthcare profession, it's important to me to provide physical comfort along with the healthcare; that's why I got into this profession to begin with. Comfort is tangible in a quilt that's made with love.

The hardest part is finding the time. I knit while I watch television, while my children are napping, or while I'm waiting. It's amazing how those little bits of time add up.

I once believed there was nothing I could do to make a difference, but I learned that all it takes is one person who takes the initiative. Thanks to my coworker's thoughtfulness, the knit-wits will keep on knitting.

Although this group started at work, a similar group could easily start from home. As long as one person coordinates, members can do their knitting at home and then give the pieces to the coordinator to put together.

Join the Club. "Join a club" doesn't always mean leaving home to attend boring meetings. These fun online clubs can help motivate us to keep giving.

- Mocha Club: <www.mochaclub.org>

- 100 Things Challenge: <www.guynameddave.com/100-thing-challenge.html>
- Junky Car Club: <www.junkycarclub.com>

Family Time

Don't forget kindnesses to your own family and friends. Our loved ones may not be starving for food, shelter, or clothes. But many are starved for time, attention, or maybe just fun. What "poverty" might the people in your life be experiencing lately?

- Alone time with Mom or Dad
- Fun time
- Rest time
- Physical affection/hugs
- Celebrations
- Smiles, positive body language
- Notes of encouragement
- Words of praise
- A dream or vision for the future
- Help with chores
- Help with homework
- Help with daunting tasks
<familyfun.go.com>
<fivelovelanguages.com>

Dinner Time

- Talk about your dreams for making a difference.
- Discuss family goals.
- Display a world map or globe in a prominent area.
- Learn about religious beliefs and customs from other cultures to better share life and faith with others.
<www.crescentproject.org>
- Talk about current events.
<www.primetimeamerica.org>.
- Memorize specific scriptures about Kingdom justice.
- Sponsor a needy child in another country. Be sure to involve the whole family in photos and letter-writing.

<www.compassion.com/amberrobinson>

- Read stories about missionaries and kids from around the world.
- Give up a night out for a fun family game time at home. Donate the extra money.
- Skip a meal. Use this as a chance to talk about world hunger.
- Adopt a missionary; then write him or her letters, and send holiday gifts.[5]

Games and Activities

- Kids of Courage—activity sheets, coloring pages, recipes, and videos

<www.kidsofcourage.com>

- Quest for Compassion—interactive game with characters who explore foreign countries and collect information.

<www.questforcompassion.org>

Birthday Party. Themes are a fun use of creativity to engage children's interests. Traditional parties often feature entertainment figures, animals, or toys. A fun spin could be to plan a themed party with a purposeful activity.

- Rock star theme

Decorations: music notes, karaoke machine, golden stars, CD's

Activity: Videotape a musical message for a sick child in the hospital.

- Military theme

Decorations: camouflage, flags, hats, maps

Activity: Create military care packages, or write letters to encourage troops and their families.

- Doll/Teddy bear theme

Decorations: dolls/Teddy bears

Activity: Build dolls/bears from ready-made parts. Give handmade items to foster children or domestic violence shelters.

<www.bdaybears.com/charity-bears.html>

- Mad Scientist

Decorations: Medical lab coats, first aid signs, toy medical gear such as stethoscopes and microscopes
Activity: Build medical supply packs for needy children in developing countries.
<www.brighthope.org/group_resources/medpacks.php?selection=home>

- Jungle Theme
Decorations: Animals, vines, plants, tropical food
Activity: Send birthday cards or care packages to missionary kids.

Holidays

- When you buy directly from the poor it gives them a chance to change their lives. Giving handmade jewelry, toys, and other items adds an extra touch of love.
<www.brighthope.com>
- Most kids make a wish list. Help your child make room on that list for a charity gift of his or her choice.
<www.smartgivers.org>
<www.charitynavigators.org>
- Donate winter apparel, household items, pantry goods, or toys to prepare your spirit for the holidays.
<www.salvationarmy.org>
- Invite an international student to share a holiday meal. In college I lived on the floor in the dorm that housed international students. I was amazed with the variety of cultures, that most of them were very interested in American customs and religious observances. This is a great opportunity for Christians to offer hospitality and share their faith. A local college will have Christian student groups who can direct you to international students.
- Take a mission trip instead of the normal theme park vacation. ServLife International will even let you pick the kind of mission trip, allowing extra rest time for families with children.
<www.servlife.org>

Give a Gift in the Name of a Family Member
- Child sponsorship, prenatal care, AIDS fund, malaria fund
<www.compassion.com>
- Animals, fishing kit, well-share, more
<www.worldvision.org>
- Clean water and wells
<www.bloodwatermission.com>
- Life-saving medical attention, bandages, surgery
<www.mercyships.org>
- Bible translation
<www.wycliffe.org>
- Jesus' life in movie form
<www.jesusfilm.org>
- Micro-enterprise loan
<www.brighthope.org/project_lists/jobcreation.php>

PERSONAL HEALTH

We can help others while doing routine healthy activities.
Donate My Weight. The Pound-for-Pound Challenge, in associa-tion with NBC's TV show "The Biggest Loser," challenges Ameri-cans to report their weight loss. For every pound lost, a pound of food is donated to food banks.
<www.pfpchallenge.com>

Ben Miller enlists his family, friends, and corporate support to pledge money or food for every pound he loses. Are you losing weight? Could you challenge friends and family to help the hun-gry?
<www.donatemyweight.com>

There's Something I Can Do—Angelina's Story

Our baby girl brought a beautiful new addition to our family four years ago. Many emotions were awakened—love, joy, and gratitude. New items were introduced—cribs, toys, diapers. As Emma grew and changed she outgrew booties, bibs, strollers, and clothes—and, like all babies, she outgrew nursing.

This left me with a freezer full of milk and a heart full of emotions. It takes a lot of effort to pump this extra milk that is a part of me, meant to be a part of her. There had to be something useful I could do with it so it didn't go to waste. I knew people could donate blood to help others; could I donate this milk to a baby who needed it?

I searched the Internet for a few hours and came up with nothing. Sadly, I threw a freezer full of breast milk away, wishing for a solution, for something better.

Two years later I was blessed with another healthy pregnancy and a baby boy. I was determined this time that I would not throw away milk.

In October 2006 I watched an Oprah feature on the International Breast Milk Project (IBMP). Jill Youse spoke about breast milk sent to Africa. My level of excitement went through the roof! I knew this was it. I had always had a heart for the needy, but didn't really know what I personally could do. The answer found me that day.

I signed up online and sent my application in to become a donor. The people on the site were so professional. They kept me up-to-date every step of the way. The organization covers shipping costs for the milk. They will also send a hospital-grade pump and storage bags for those who need them. I arranged for postal pickups of milk shipments from home. IBMP's attention to detail was impressive. Their screening process ensured that only healthy milk made its way overseas.

I became even more involved by becoming a chapter president and began coordinating fundraisers. My life changed. I was living out something I believed in. I even got to meet a man from South Africa who had seen firsthand the urgent need for these shipments. I knew after speaking with him that we did not just transport milk—we sent hope.

I struggle to fit everything into my busy schedule: my kids, my husband, my friends, and my household tasks. Life runs at full speed. I won't pretend that I don't wonder sometimes if I can keep up.

But then I see firsthand the impact on my children. My little girl prays at night, *Thank you for Mommy, Daddy, Brother, cheeseburgers, and the little boys and girls in Africa.*
<www.breastmilkproject.org>
What we can learn from Angelina's story is *persistence*. She knew she wanted to help but didn't quite know how. It took an idea, some research, and some time to find her passion.

Obstacles to Helping

Angelina's obstacle was locating the right charity. There will be roadblocks as we search for ways to help others. Be prepared to keep moving in the right direction toward mercy and grace.

Here are some common obstacles:

• Anxiety
• Lack of time
• Lack of money
• Lack of social support
• Compassion fatigue
• Meager results
• Physical illness or limitation

I understand the obstacle of physical limitation. In the past, recurring health issues devoured weeks and months of my life. Obstacles cause us to feel useless and unable to help in any measurable way. But being homebound, I find prayer to be a powerful detour around any hindrances. I open my laptop and gather prayer requests from mission organizations, pastors, and news agencies. Sometimes the organization reports a powerful answer—sometimes nothing. But I know I contribute vital aid to that ministry.

PRAYER

Not prayer! I inwardly groan. *Give me something "practical"!*
I wear out the word "prayer" until my eyes glaze over. Familiarity strips away my ability to see the profound. Gravity no longer seems noteworthy, but without it I would cease to live. In the same way, all my spiritual efforts cease to have life without prayer.

At some point in your life you'll be homebound. You might be home with a toddler, an illness, or a disability. Don't give up! You're a valuable member of the Kingdom justice team.

Obstacles Demolished

Those who are very active and think that they are going to encircle the earth with their preaching . . . should realize that they would do the Church much more good, and please God much more . . . if they spend even half of this time being with God in prayer. . . . In this way they would certainly achieve more with less trouble in one work than they would have done in a thousand (John of the Cross).

When we pray we knock on the gates of heaven. With the intensity of mighty thunder, the spiritual realm is shaken, and the world is changed. We gain access to the King of Kings and Lord of Lords.

"I say to you: Ask and it will be given to you; seek and you will find; knock and the door will be opened to you" (Luke 11:9).

Is prayer hard? Does it require us to be a bit more disciplined? Does real change seem elusive most of the time? Yes, but keep going. Those few treasured moments of answered prayers make it worthwhile. No matter who we are, we can pray.

Prayer Resources

- <www.operationworld.org>
- <www.prayovertheworld.org>
- <www.missionaryweb.com>
- Your local church's Web site
- Charity web page (see Appendix)

Home Aid

Mother Teresa said people should begin in their own homes to remedy poverty. Her prescription to love grates against the culture of grand gestures that tells us to serve where we'll be seen. I pour out myself for others' praise. I sweat beneath the heat of a spotlight.

But ask me to choose to answer with kind words.

To revisit my online shopping habits.

To cook a meal for the sick.

To donate my business suit when it is so much easier to throw it away.

To turn off the television to pray.

How will I respond?

Reflect

1. Have you ever thought about making a difference from home?

2. At this point in your life, how much time do you spend at home? Is it realistic to try something from the lists?

3. Can you identify with the common obstacles to helping? Which one of the following hinders you the most? Anxiety, time, money, social support, compassion fatigue, meager results, physical limitations.

4. It is our tendency to want to try everything at once. Why is it important to find *one* new thing?

5. What idea did you like best from each section?
   Computer
   Housework
   Hobbies
   Family time
   Personal health
   Prayer

6. Can you focus on *one* thing you can do from home?

PART II
The One Thing I Can Do

SHOPPING

The Laws of Clothes Shopping—
If you like it, they don't have it in your size.
If you like it and it fits, you can't afford it.
If you like it, it fits, and you can afford it,
it falls apart the first time you wear it.
If the shoe fits, it's ugly.

Today's news—political images splashed across pages like so much wet paint, not quite dry in my mind before the next image of the hour appears.

Politicians vie for your vote on election day. Surveys seek your opinion on everything from what television shows you watch to what laundry detergent you use.

We vote, we comment on blogs, and we participate in surveys. But our most powerful influence can be found in what we buy.

With every dollar spent, I'm supporting the companies that run the world. My purchases provide the funds to employ their workers, support their political leanings, and invest in local communities. Companies set wages, hours, and conditions for their workers. Every dollar they make in turn pays numerous vendors, marketing teams, and insurance companies. When I make a purchase I send the message "Strive for quality at a fair price" or "Continue to cut corners in ethics, health, and safety." I reflect my values through my purchases, whether or not I do so intentionally.

The fast food children's meal we purchase or the jar of spaghetti sauce we add to the shopping cart seems insignificant. But what if we added up the jars of sauce in the houses in just one neighborhood? What difference could it make if those families changed one purchase? My single purchase combined with millions of other households is a cog, moving gears in a financial machine that either contributes to life or tears it down.

You may be wondering if what you purchase really makes a difference. Besides, who needs one more thing to think about? But what you purchase *does* make a difference, and there are some groups doing amazing research and bringing to light the business practices of companies. Weigh your options. The impact the buying public has on the success or demise of a product or retail entity is huge.

Love it or hate it, we spend a lot of time shopping. We buy groceries, clothes, gifts, entertainment, home goods, and much more. I've struggled with shopping. Sometimes I absolutely love it. Sometimes I feel guilty. How much is okay? What's excessive? What's the right standard? There are few easy answers.

We can start shopping strategically. When I know my small purchase benefits the welfare of an employee, contributes to the health of my family, and is cost effective, shopping is much more enjoyable.

Shop Locally

My family obsesses over our *Little House on the Prairie* DVD set. It's actually pretty goofy. When we watch this 1970s television series, we crack up at audio errors, the simple special effects, and sappy story lines. So why do we continue to watch?

Something inside us tells us we missed out by not living in this historical time period when we would have known the local merchants by name, supported our neighbor's small business, and lived life together with family and community. I wouldn't want to give up electricity, and I'm too sissy to be a pioneer, but I long for a better way to do life and business. Nostalgia aside, there are great economic, health, and social benefits to shopping locally.

Local shoppers give their business to merchants who are close to home and members of the community. The majority of local businesses are not a part of big chains. You can search for local merchants online by business type or by location. Despite the debate[1] over buying local, the benefits[2] win out.

Benefits of Shopping Locally

- More flavorful, nutrient-dense, fresh food that contains fewer pesticides and antibiotics
- Preservation of open farmland
- Business dealings with a "real person"
- Fair wages for farmers and employees by cutting out middleman suppliers
- Savings in time and gas as you shop close to home
- Promotion of growth for the local economy—the "multiplier effect" begins as money is circulated in the town you live in. If just ten percent of purchases in San Francisco alone were directed back to local business, 1,300 jobs would be created and $200 million dollars of revenue would be generated.[3]
- Increase in local tax revenue
- Availability of discount coupons in local newspapers and flyers

Where to Shop

- Your own home garden
  <www.aerogrow.com>
  <www.kitchengardeners.org>
  <www.squarefootgardening.com>
  <www.yourbackyardfarmer.com>
- Your own front door—fresh produce delivered directly to your home
  <www.farmfreshdelivery.com>
- A local drop-off site—Community Supported Agriculture (CSA) allows the consumer to buy a "share" of farm products, keeping prices low. You won't have to drive thirty to fifty miles to the farm. Produce is brought to a location near you.

<www.localharvest.org>
• Farmer's markets and produce stands
<www.farmersmarket.com>
• Local establishments such as bakeries, restaurants, florists, and hair salons
<www.eatwellguide.org>
• Another interesting concept is a "justice kitchen." Eat great food, have fun, and learn more about local food.
<www.friendsofwfp.org>

Grace Garden—Sara's Story

I wish I could turn my entire backyard into a giant garden. My husband wouldn't budge. I have a suburban lot, and my four-by-four-foot garden patch blends into the landscaping. Gardens pull at something deep within me. They call to the part of my soul that is wild and free in the outdoors. They give me confidence that I'm sending safe nutrition to the baby growing within me. But most important of all, gardens beckon to me from days past, when people came together to laugh, work, and eat good food.

I noticed that our church has a huge unused patch of land in the back. A farmer rents part of it for a corn crop, but there's still plenty of space. I had the idea to start a garden. I didn't really know what I was getting myself into when the outreach director said, "Go for it."

We called it the "Grace Garden," derived from part of our church's name. An architect church member drew up the plans, we ordered the seeds, and when it was time to break ground, we rounded up some rotary tillers and were ready to start.

It was a soggy, messy, muddy May. Coordinating the volunteers was a big job because of the fickle thunderclouds. It was almost comedic to see how far we could get before we ran for cover from the lightning. Thanks to a great group effort, we finally finished twelve rows.

One beautiful summer afternoon the sky cleared, and I found myself tilling the ground alone. I was hoping for a team of helpers, but God had something else in mind. I unloaded the tiller, scratching a gash into my SUV paneling—whoops, sorry hubby—and ended up completing six rows. There's something soul-satisfying to look back and see the physical manifestation of sweaty work. Work in my office sometimes takes weeks or months to finish. Here I could see the progress, touch it, and give thanks for it. I was physically spent and spiritually full.

We learned a lot from our start-up year and will be making lots of improvements. We're delegating work to plot leaders for increased efficiency. We're bringing in local agriculture educators to teach gardening skills to church members and the surrounding community. Last year's inner-city children helpers are working on their own garden in their youth center so they have something beautiful right where they live. Our produce feeds church families and supplies produce to a local food pantry and women's center.

Coordinating our volunteers with the whims of Mother Nature seems nearly impossible. But when I see gardening families working and laughing together, when I see communities educated and gaining access to healthy and affordable food, I know it's well worth it. Lives changed—the fruit and vegetables of our work, God's goodness and love in our garden of His grace.

<www.gracegarden.wordpress.com>

Small changes last over time. A big change that ends next Tuesday is not real change. When Aaron and I were first married, he was regularly consuming high-sugar beverages and fast food. I ate lots of frozen and box meals. If we had overhauled our diets immediately, we might not still be married; we both love food! Aaron went from soda to juice and now to water as his main source of hydration. I went from box mixes to using a slow cooker to incorporating herbs and vegetables into our meals. This evolution is still happening, and it has taken years of change—one habit at a time.

SHOP SMART

Better Products

What about products you can't buy locally? What about on-line purchases? How do you know what companies and products to support? The Internet eliminates long hours of research—someone else has done the busy work for us. Ranking guides are the way to go to search by product or brand name and have instant access to great information.

Better World Shopper <www.betterworldshopper.org>

- The Web site: report-card-style rankings in seventy-five categories
- The shopping guide: report-card-style rankings in a pocket-sized book
- The digital guide: download it to a digital device to take with you on the go

Good Guide <www.goodguide.com>

- The Web site: food, personal care, cleaners, and toys rated on a ten-point scale with pop-up windows that give details about the rating
- The discussion board: an opportunity to chat with other guide users and to post ideas
- The product safety and recalls list: latest updates and information
- The products' political ties: Is your purchase supporting red or blue?
- The digital guide: for mobile phone or texting

Mercy Rising <www.mercyrising.blogspot.com>

- Shop smart from a Christian worldview

Considerations: Find out why a product has a certain ranking. Don't just take their word for it. Don't assume that a particular Web site ranks items the same way you would.

Calculate the Hidden Costs

No one wants to miss out on a good deal. But what's the full cost beyond the price tag?

- Health: What are the long-term costs of food, household cleaners, and personal care items? What will it cost in time, energy, and medical bills if those products cause long-term damage to your family? Safer alternatives save more than money over time.
- Quality: How long will this product last? Will my plumber fix the leak the first time? Save time and money by not constantly having to replace items.

  <www.consumerreports.org>

  <www.angieslist.com>
- Ethics: Bad business wreaks havoc on the economy and ruins lives. See the Book of Proverbs for promised blessing to the wise person and forecasted disaster to the foolish. Supporting companies with good records of ethics makes sense for personal finances and overall economic prosperity.

  Corp Ethics

  <www.corp-ethics.com>

  This corporate watchdog keeps consumers up to date on practices that branch out beyond human rights, to include fraud, litigation, and misleading advertising.

  Open Secrets

  <www.opensecrets.org>

  This comprehensive online database allows searches to disclose political donations and lobbying. Search by individual donor name, or go to the heavy-hitters section to see what your products support by checking up on the companies that produce them.
- Peace of mind
- Human life: Slavery is not just sex-trafficking. For every sex slave there are fifteen domestic labor or agriculture slaves, although some workers are both.[4] These horrific abuses are abhorrent in the sight of God.

What are sweatshops? Some think they are only urban legends, but they exist. Most are found overseas, but some operate illegally in large cities in the United States. In 2004 a Department of Labor investigation traced sweatshop products to well-known stores such as J. C. Penney, Kohls, Sears, Target, and Wal-Mart.[5]

If sweatshop-produced items are in many stores, what should we do? There's no foolproof method to eliminate these purchases from our lives, but these may give you a better chance:

- Buy high-quality items.
- Buy local.
- Buy items made in the United States.
- Buy fair trade items.
- Spark change with consumer pressure through letter-writing campaigns and product boycotts.

Don't underestimate consumer pressure. One company that had made a notorious "Public Eye Award" list for human rights violations a few years ago has turned its act around to receive above-average marks in a 2008 report.[6] Check and make sure your information is current and correct before writing letters or boycotting products.

Here are some great Web sites:

Chain Store Reaction

<www.chaistorereaction.com>

Chain Store Reaction discloses company diligence to cut ties to the slave trade. This user-friendly site allows you to click on a logo for its rating. If your brand has not posted a disclosure policy, a sample request is linked to send. If your brand is not listed, request it to be added.

Clean Clothes Campaign

<www.cleanclothes.org>

This campaign's goal is to improve working conditions in the global garment industry. This site is informative as it publishes yearly reports that rate and describe clothing company practices. But it's also emotional to read real women's stories of deplorable working conditions. Ironically, it's women's clothing purchases that are unknowingly destroying the lives of many other women who make these garments.

Is the extra effort worth it? Does changing one purchase make a difference? An American worker stays safe on the job and receives adequate health care. He or she contributes to the economy through purchases and taxes. He or she does not need unemployment, Social Security, disability, or other social services. His or her children receive a good education.

The cycle of poverty is broken.

A south Asian farmer sustains himself by his work. He does not sell himself or his children into slavery for food. He does not need to borrow from the moneylenders or pay off debt.

The cycle of poverty is broken.

The laborer, the company, the merchant, the shopper—dignity restored for each.

SHOP FAIR

What is a fair trade product?
According to TransFairUSA it includes—
- Fair wages
- Fair labor conditions: safe working conditions, a livable wage, and no child labor
- Direct trade: elimination of middlemen to keep prices low
- Democratic and transparent organization: decision-making as a group
- Community development: reinvestment in development and improvements
- Environmental sustainability: healthy, sustainable food and farming practice[7]

When I see the "Fair Trade Certified" logo, I know that a thorough evaluation process ensures a profitable livelihood to those who provide my food. I enjoy long-term benefits of safer, more healthful food. Doing the right thing is good for everyone.

What products can be certified for fair trade?
- cocoa and chocolate

- coffee
- cotton
- flowers and plants (fresh)
- fruits and vegetables (dried and fresh)
- fruit juice
- herbs and spices
- nuts
- olives and olive oil
- quinoa
- rice
- soy
- sugar and honey
- tea
- vanilla

More products will become eligible for fair trade certification. For current listings visit <www.transfairusa.org>.

Which stores carry fair trade products?

The Fair Trade Certified site will allow you to search by state, city, or zip code to find local and national merchants in your area: <www.transfairusa.org/content/WhereToBuy>. The listing will also let you know which type of fair trade products those merchants supply. Retailers include natural food stores, cafés, and national chain grocery stores.

Why are some items marked fair trade without the certification seal?

Certification does not exist for every product. This means digging to find out if a company's labeling is misleading or if products really support those in poverty who are rebuilding their lives through sustainable business.

Christian sites

- Bright Hope International: coffee, jewelry, gifts, home items <www.brighthope.com>
- Christian Freedom International: paper, jewelry, clothes, home items; aids the persecuted church.

<www.christianhandcrafts.com>
- Cards from Africa: cards, calendars, paper
<www.cardsfromafrica.com>

General fair trade sites
- World of Good: wide variety of items with well-marked labeling and source information
<http://worldofgood.ebay.com>
- Fair Trade Federation: informative site about fair trade with a comprehensive search feature that lets you browse by product or category
<www.fairtradefederation.org>

SHOP EXTRA

Now that we know where to shop and what products make sense, what about others around us? This shopping strategy is so easy. Just pick up extra items to have on hand for those in need:
- Extra can of food
- Extra bag of groceries
- Extra meal: College students donate unused meals from university dining plans.[8]
- Extra coupons: Expired coupons don't expire for military families.
<www.couponing.about.com/cs/aboutcouponing/a/militaryexpcoup.html>
- Extra gift card balance: Do you have an odd amount, like $1.06, left on a gift card? Give your unused balance to make a big difference.
<www.giftcarddonor.com>
- Extra medical supplies
<www.brighthope.org/group_resources/medpacks.php>
- Extra school supplies
<www.brighthope.org/group_resources/hopepacks.php>
<www.backpackattackindy.org>
- Extra shoes
<www.shoesfororphansouls.org>

- Extra denim: Old denim is recycled for insulation in low-income housing.
  <www.cottonfrombluetogreen.org>
- Extra jeans: Teens start jeans drives at school to help homeless kids. Clothing stores periodically serve as drop-off points and will offer discounts for newly purchased jeans.
  <www.dosomething.org/teensforjeans/take-action>
- Extra holiday gifts
Angel Tree
  <www.angeltree.org>
Operation Christmas Child
  <www.samaritanspurse.org/index.php/OCC/index/>
- Extra mile: We often focus so much on charities that we forget the real people in our lives. An extra bag of groceries, a gift card, or a babysitting offer goes a long way.

One Can Make a Difference—Hope's Story

My small piece in the justice puzzle is organizing our local food collection. Each Saturday morning volunteers arrive at church ready for the food collection.

We disperse teams of two or three to local groceries and stand outside their front doors with flyers. We let local patrons know that we're collecting one canned good for the local food pantry. Even though we live in the suburbs, hunger is very real here. Our local food bank's shelves empty before the week's end. Later the teams return to church and pack the food into crates, and one driver drops the food off at the local food bank.

It's exciting to see the reactions of store patrons. A young couple who had once used the very same food bank found a way to donate. A man who went inside for a soda came out with two boxes of food for donation.

One blustery cold morning I raced over to the church. A volunteer had cancelled, and I didn't have anyone else scheduled to help. I was so surprised to walk into a busy parking lot. Random volunteers unexpectedly showed up, and the process ran smoothly.

Just as God provides for the hungry, He provides workers for the task. I'm so grateful for those faithful volunteers who advance Kingdom work, one Saturday, one store, one can of food at a time.

<www.gracecc.org/hamilton-county-food-pantry-drive/>
<www.foodrescue.net>

SHOP TOGETHER

- Friends can buy in bulk to save money.
- The elderly, sick, or disabled: take them with you.
- Family: teach children wise shopping and giving practices.
- Store employees: treat them kindly, and thank them for their assistance.

SHOP FAST

By "shop fast," I don't mean shopping at the speed of light. I mean "fast" as in fasting, taking a break, or pausing. Fasting is voluntarily abstaining for a specified time to re-center on spiritual life through prayer. It retunes our dependence on God instead of on objects.

When is hitting all the best sales thrifty, and when does it cross the line into being downright obsessive? We wouldn't be the first women to have trouble keeping our possessions from drowning us.

The LORD says, "The women of Zion are haughty, walking along with outstretched necks, flirting with their eyes, tripping along with mincing steps, with ornaments jingling on their ankles. Therefore the Lord will bring sores on the heads of the women of Zion; the LORD will make their scalps bald."

In that day the Lord will snatch away their finery: the bangles and headbands and crescent necklaces, the earrings and bracelets and veils, the headdresses and ankle chains and sashes, the perfume bottles and charms, the signet rings and nose rings, the fine robes and the capes and cloaks, the purses and mirrors, and the linen garments and tiaras and shawls.

Instead of fragrance there will be a stench; instead of a sash, a rope; instead of well-dressed hair, baldness; instead of fine clothing, sackcloth; instead of beauty, branding. Your men will fall by the sword, your warriors in battle. The gates of Zion will lament and mourn; destitute, she will sit on the ground (*Isaiah 3:16-26*).

Human devastation is real. Zion women swam in the waters of their stuff when the tsunami struck that day. What kind of God would let that happen? Actually He did not just let it happen—the Lord did it himself. Why? Zion was the community of His beloved—His chosen people, His daughters.

Imagine with me that every fine piece of clothing, accessory, and jewelry was instead heavy weights, chains, and ropes. Those gals were treading water, but the heavy objects were pulling them down; the current was sweeping them out to sea, and they were in real danger.

God as heroic champion steps in to save the women. He pulls off ropes, cuts through chains, and releases the weights. He aches with the women as they sink to the shore and weep. He loves them and wraps unseen comfort around their spirits. Sometimes we, like the Zion women, mourn our losses. But would we really prefer to drown under the weight of what we once had?

To want more is to be human. I crave comfort in books, music, clothes, and technology. I forget that all I own is temporary. It's passing away.

Unfortunately, Zion's purchases weren't just hurting themselves.

> The LORD enters into judgment against the elders and leaders of his people: "It is you who have ruined my vineyard; the plunder from the poor is in your houses.
>
> What do you mean by crushing my people and grinding the faces of the poor?" declares the Lord, the LORD Almighty (*Isaiah 3.14-15*).

Both the men and women were pulling the poor down with them. They were getting rich at the expense of others.

I own dishes collecting dust in cupboards, boxed items in the garage, clothing hung in closets. These were things I shouldn't have bought in the first place but can't quite give away; things I've bought with the wrong motives; things I bought at a cheap price at the expense of a worker's fair wage and working in unsanitary conditions. What else could be found in our homes? Is it the plunder from the poor?

Maybe we need a "shop fast"—a pause, a reflection, a break.

Liberating Lent

The Lenten season is traditionally the forty days before Easter. We prepare our hearts for the coming of Resurrection Sunday. Sometimes we use this season as a reminder to take a break from consumerism and consumption. But we can take time out from our stuff anytime, not just during Lent.

What has a hold on your heart right now? Do you need a break?

- Clothes
- Electronic devices
- Entertainment products
- Certain foods
- Home décor/improvement items
- Restaurant foods/take out
- Children's toys

Alternatives

Replace the time spent shopping with something better. Many people say they wish they had more time. What would you do? Would you read, play a musical instrument, learn another language, paint, cook, or learn to dance? Invite others to join in the fun. You can reconnect and have a blast.

Maybe you wish you had more time to meditate and read Scripture. The fast re-centers and balances your life.

Break the Fast

Once the fast is over, it's time to start living in moderation. Walk in freedom, leaving the guilt behind. When in doubt, here are some questions to ask when shopping:

- Am I spending within the guidelines of a predetermined budget?

- Would my spouse—if applicable—approve?
- Am I trending toward downsizing or upscaling?
- What is my motivation?
- How has my giving been this month?
- Have I prayed about it?

A Better Ending

When we last saw the Zion women, they were mourning their losses; they were devastated. But the Lord did not leave them there:

> In that day the Branch of the LORD will be beautiful and glorious, and the fruit of the land will be the pride and glory of the survivors in Israel. Those who are left in Zion, who remain in Jerusalem, will be called holy, all who are recorded among the living in Jerusalem. The Lord will wash away the filth of the women of Zion; he will cleanse the bloodstains from Jerusalem by a spirit of judgment and a spirit of fire. Then the LORD will create over all of Mount Zion and over those who assemble there a cloud of smoke by day and a glow of flaming fire by night; over all the glory will be a canopy. It will be a shelter and shade from the heat of the day, and a refuge and hiding place from the storm and rain (*Isaiah 4:2-6*).

The water that washed the fine goods away cleansed their spirits. The glory of the Lord surrounded them with

mercy
love
protection
beauty.

REFLECTION

1. Do you like to shop? Why or why not?

2. Name five recent purchases and retailers.

3. Did you use any of the following techniques in shopping for those purchases? Which area is your strength? Which area is your weakness?
   Shop local.
   Shop smart.
   Shop fair.
   Shop extra.
   Shop together.
   Shop fast.

4. Pick one item to rate at <www.goodguide.com>. What was the score?

5. In what areas do you tend to overspend? Do you need a break?

6. Has God taken away things that proved harmful? Can you relate to the women of Zion? Can you see His mercy, love, protection, or beauty?

7. What is the *one* thing you want to change in your shopping habits?

IT'S JUST BUSINESS

Finance is our seed sown into the lives of people.
—Angela Sah[1]

Most of us spend forty to sixty or more hours each week working. Whether we commute to an office in a high rise, change diapers, or manage a small business, we spend most of our waking hours industriously. I don't usually feel that owning my own business changes the world. It just seems like hard work.

We face demanding schedules, colleagues, and supervisors or feel strained by resources, time, and substandard staff. With those distractions, how can we make a difference at work?

Whatever you do, work at it with all your heart, as working for the Lord, not for men, since you know that you will receive an inheritance from the Lord as a reward. It is the Lord Christ you are serving (*Colossians 3:23-25*).

What does that really look like when not everyone believes it? God is calling us to reconnect spiritual life to everyday life—through our commutes, business networks, knowledge and skills, treatment of employees, ethics practices, and business models.

COMMUTING

More than 128 million people commute to work.[2] We may imagine only those in big cities come across the poor during their commutes, but that's not true. We can assist a stranded motorist, the hungry, a member of a "tent city,"[3] or those temporarily displaced by natural disasters. Often we're on the way somewhere, so our interaction time is limited. What preparations can we take for meaningful connections?

Lovebags—Chelsea's story

It started three years ago when my college friends and I noticed some hungry people on the beach. We decided the least we could do was round up some food. We took peanut-butter-and-jelly sandwiches mixed with a little uncertainty, and off we went. We met Steve, who was holding a sign on a busy street corner and "adopted" him. It was a lot of work for us. About ten of us were always on call. Did we really think we had a chance to get him off the streets? We listened to him, paid for his car, fed him, and helped him find a job. Over the course of three months he became a Christian and left his life of drugs. He now lives in his own apartment and takes in other homeless people.

There were three crucial components to "real help:" the relentless love of Jesus, a community that believed in him, and practical assistance.

The peanut-butter-and-jelly sandwiches evolved into love-bags, pre-packed items used to interact with someone in need. You can go to the Web site to find a group in your area, or you can start one on your own. Lovebags also partners with local coffee shops, restaurants, churches, and individuals who want to make a difference in their communities.

Helping the poor isn't something I do—it's a way of living out who I am. I connect with the homeless because I see myself in them. They have physical needs they cannot hide. We have spiritual needs we do our best to hide. We all have addictions—theirs just happen to bring them here.
<www.lovebags.org>

Build Your Own Lovebag
- Water bottle
- Canned tuna that requires no can opener; dried jerky; chicken pouch
- Single-serve applesauce or other fruit
- Granola bar
- Plastic spoon

- Personal care items: toothbrush, toothpaste, floss
- Address/information on local food banks, shelters, and churches that have programs for the homeless
- Handwritten note of love and concern
- Gospel of John book, plan of salvation booklet

Seasonal items

- Summer: rain poncho
- Winter: scarf, mittens, or hat

Put in as many or as few items as you wish. The size of the bags will vary. A small plastic bag fits into a coat pocket. Store larger lovebags in your car. Also, don't assume all people who need help are literate. Some require further assistance.

General Guidelines

- Allow the Holy Spirit to lead you. We can't help everyone, but we can help some.
- Be safe. Women are best at interacting with other women or children in the daytime or in well-lit areas.
- Take time to hear their stories. Walk with them to get a meal.
- Call or direct them to an agency for long-term assistance.

Be Forewarned

Giving money to someone without knowing the situation can do more harm than good, as it may encourage bad work habits, substance abuse, or deceitful gain. Or even worse, it could aid illegal slave trafficking in which abusers exploit victims as beggars.[4]

Does that mean we should never give money? Not necessarily, but we should lean on the guidance of the Holy Spirit, being careful not to undo the work of organizations that encourage rehabilitation and transformation.[5]

Networking and Encouragement

Our pastor recently spoke about giving joyfully in hard times. His basic premise was that even when the world around us melts in fear, Christians should give generously—even when it hurts. Before the service, he had random people in the congregation hand out candy to unsuspecting fellow churchgoers. It was an experiment of sorts. Would we share the candy with those around us, or would we keep it all for ourselves? During his sermon, he polled the crowd to find out how many did and did not receive candy. Then he had one of the candy-less members join him up front.

He prayed for the man, saying, "Lord, we pray for our brother. He's got a lot of need with his candy and we're just praying that one of his rich candy friends would bless him with all the candy he'd ever need. We feel terrible that no one shared with him, and we just pray that you'd help him. In Jesus' name, Amen." The funny visual burnt into our brains: the pastor laid one hand on his friend's shoulder while clutching his own big bag of candy in the other. As the crowd burst into laughter, he instructed the man to sit down. He then commented to the laughing crowd that we do the same thing with our money to those in need. Silence.[6]

Later that week many people who heard that same sermon asked my job-seeking husband, "Let me know if you need anything." While thankful for concern, the situation was a little awkward. We've said the same thing to others, clueless many times. But it got me thinking.

Call and response.

"How are you?"

"I'm fine."

Volley and return.

"Let me know if you need anything."

"Thanks—I will."

We play the etiquette game on autopilot. Instead of asking "if," we could offer specific help. The best kind results in work. Can you connect the job-seeker to your contacts? Networking is as important as a good résumé.

Another way is financial help, but it encourages or humiliates, depending on how it's done. Small amounts of cash won't salvage bankruptcy but can extend an emotional lifeline. Giving can also be anonymous. This keeps the recipient from feeling beholden to the giver. I've often signed my name to charitable gifts but am just now starting to be sensitive about when it is or is not appropriate.

Each situation is different. A better tag line might be "From a fellow worshiper, member at _____ church [or "Christ-follower"]."

"Let us not love [merely] in theory or in speech but in deed and in truth (in practice and in sincerity)" (1 John 3:18, AMP).

Some Ways You Can Help People Who Are Out of Work

- Network. Pass their résumé or business card to someone who's hiring.
- Connect them with a local church for encouragement and practical help.
- Suggest a time bank, a Web site that connects people with other service providers. Participants accrue "points" by rendering a service to someone else in the system. When you need a provider, you spend your "points." The web site manages and keeps the system running. No time bank in your area? Start/organize one in your city. <www.timebanks.org>
- Send money, a grocery gift card, or a prepaid bank card.
- Cut them a break if you're a service provider—legal services, repair jobs, child care, medical care—reduce their bill this month by facilitating a sale or providing a discount coupon.
- Babysit their kids for free, especially during job interviews.
- Do fun stuff with them—have dinner together, plan some activity, or just hang out.
- Provide movie tickets for the family. Comedy is a great stress relief.

Things you can say:

- "How was your week?" That's an open-ended question. If they want to talk about the job search, fine; if not, it doesn't put them on the spot.
- Avoid any words or action to make them feel like a project or "charity case."

Business Skills

There are other ways you can help with your professional skills. In the professional realm of helping others, we often think of those with degrees in counseling, social work, theology, and so on. But skills in every field are needed for Kingdom justice. You can use your skills directly with those in need, or you can benefit nonprofits behind the scenes.

Here are a few categories of skills needed in Kingdom justice work:

- Art and music—promote causes in concerts and events[7]
- Auto repair
- Professional driving—transporting large groups of people
- Business management
- Clerical work—volunteer from home or on-site
- Food preparation—cook for shelters, camps, events, food reclamation,
  <www.secondhelpings.org>
  <www.soallmayeat.org>
- Computer technology—create Web sites, databases, graphics
  <www.geekcorps.org>
- Construction—rebuild houses, complete projects for seniors or those in need
  <www.plain-o-helpers.org>
  <www.habitat.org>
- Education—teach English overseas, aid mission work, promote literacy
  <www.elic.org>
  <www.cefonline.com>
- ngineering—rebuild villages, design infrastructure
  <www.ewb-usa.org>
- Finance—file taxes, manage accounts, design financial plans
  <www.cvas-usa.org>
  <www.crown.org>
- Healthcare—serve in clinics or medical missions
  <www.shepherdcommunity.org/programs/clinic>
  <www.mercyships.org>
- Human resources—mobilize people for projects or fundraisers, teach job skills

- Legal counsel—advise organizations or needy clients
  <www.clsnet.org>
  <www.nclegalclinic.org>
- Marketing—fundraise, write a grant, promote a cause
- Real estate—create a foundation to combat homelessness
  <www.mibor.com/realtorfoundation/about.asp>
- Writing—compose newsletters, press releases, grants

"More Than"—Stephanie's Story

"I don't have to be here. You can't make me. You're not my momma!"

Sasha is one tough cookie. She glares from the back of the classroom. Her sassy exterior hides a world of hurt. Feeling out of place, she fights back, and right now that anger is aimed at me. The others watch as I say, "I would love to have you join in, but that's fine." She can't argue with me if I don't engage her. I redirect my attention to the class. "Good. Can you explain to me how you got that answer? Now we're going to learn some shortcuts to help you get done quicker."

"What's that you're doing?" Sasha asks. She is hooked and starts completing the problems along with the class.

Fast-forward a month. Sasha, a student in danger of failing, turns in her homework. She raises her hand, ready with the correct answers. In a few weeks she's not only learning but teaching classmates. As confidence soars, negative behaviors start to fall away.

Today she ran to put her arms around my neck and almost started to cry with happiness. Sasha tested the highest in her class. Her teacher confirmed her advancement to the next math grade level. Her aunt and uncle planned a very special reward for her new achievements.

This is not just a job—it's my calling. Along with my teaching and tutoring, I also attend various school activities so the students know I really care about them, not just their academic progress.

Not every child is a success story. Keeton, once a top student, is now going to be a father before he reaches ninth grade. Outcomes like this are heart-wrenching. But I have to keep reaching out, doing what I can, and giving children the skills to succeed. There's nothing better than seeing God at work when I look into the eyes of lost children and see that they realize that someone cares about them no matter what they do or say.

INFLUENCE, ACCESS, AND RESOURCES

Depending on what company you work for, you may have connections to coworkers and resources that can be used for good. If a group of coworkers becomes energized, that energy sustains and motivates the group not to give up. Excitement builds as the group looks forward to further participation.

Influence

What products does your company purchase? Does the business partner with charitable organizations? One company's actions influence employees and other businesses to get involved.

- Coffee, paper products, office supplies from fair trade organizations
- Cleaning supplies that are healthful for the cleaning staff and other employees
- Furniture from eco-conscious groups
- Paper recycling
- Technology recycling if applicable
- Corporate sponsorship for charity events
- Cause of the year—statistics in the company newsletter, a company-wide contest for volunteerism, or holiday drive
- Logo or link to the partner charity on the company Web site

Access

These are donations that businesses can make that would not necessarily constitute a financial contribution. In some cases a donation of this type may mean a tax-deduction for the business. Some ideas may include—

- Delivery truck use (for food or heavy items)

- Special seats at events
- Conference rooms or meeting space for charities
- Surplus office supplies
- Office furniture or fixtures after a renovation <www.givesomethingback.com>
- Replaced technology
- Leftover food given to a food bank from meetings or parties
- Goods produced by the business
- Pro-bono services

Resources

- Corporate sponsorship
- Paid time off to volunteer
- Company reimbursement for expenses incurred when employees volunteer
- Company matches on employee contributions
- The option to choose a socially responsible investment fund <www.socialinvest.org>
- Money for time—a donation of a certain amount of money per volunteer hour.[8]

Small Steps

Just because you're really excited about a partnership does not mean everyone else will be. Start small. Ask the human resources manager what programs are already in place, and join in those efforts. If you want to start something new, offer to do the busy work to get the project going. Be polite and persistent. Emphasize the benefits to the company. Utilize Web sites that will organize, motivate, and help coordinate volunteer efforts. Find a partnership that is mutually beneficial with clearly defined expectations by both parties.
<www.angelpoints.com>

Workers in Business

We all want to be treated fairly by management where we work, but sometimes we don't think about how we treat the boss. Ethics go both ways.

- Work hard for your company.
- Do menial tasks with enthusiasm and completion.
- Cut costs and resist the urge to take company items.
- Tell the truth about wages and earnings.
- Combat negative stereotypes that employees are lazy and disrespectful.

ENTREPRENEURS AND BUSINESS OWNERS

"The Christ who was born in poverty got His initial start-up capital from three wealthy businessmen" (Robert Lupton).

The Old Testament has some great instructions about the relationship between business owners and the poor. While Christians don't strictly follow the laws of Judaism, we can still learn from their justice practices.

Case Study One: Boaz Model

"When you reap the harvest of your land, do not reap to the very edges of your field or gather the gleanings of your harvest" (Leviticus 19:9).

> When you are harvesting in your field and you overlook a sheaf, do not go back to get it. Leave it for the alien, the fatherless and the widow, so that the LORD your God may bless you in all the work of your hands.
>
> When you beat the olives from your trees, do not go over the branches a second time. Leave what remains for the alien, the fatherless and the widow.
>
> When you harvest the grapes in your vineyard, do not go over the vines again. Leave what remains for the alien, the fatherless and the widow.
>
> Remember that you were slaves in Egypt. That is why I command you to do this (*Deuteronomy 24:19-22*).

The basic Boaz principle set up a framework in which the poor could work to provide for their families. This not only benefited the needy family, but the landowner also kept excessive greed in check. The Lord wanted them to remember where they came from—slavery. Only then would they be able to show mercy to others.

The story of the landowner, Boaz, is often told only as a love story. In the midst of a human love story is God's love story for a widow and an immigrant daughter-in-law. Boaz was a wealthy landowner who was in the practice of caring for those in need. What can we learn from his story?

- Boaz was a good manager.
- He was respected by his employees and he treated them well.
- He followed the gleaning laws and let his fields be worked by the poor.
- He showed favor on Ruth for her hard work and allowed her an extra harvest, access to water, and ensured her safety by preventing wayward advances from the workmen.
- God used Boaz's faithfulness to give the characters in the story a double blessing as he married Ruth, breaking the yoke of poverty for this family.

This is no ordinary love story. Boaz, as the "kinsman redeemer," is a forerunner of Jesus' redeeming us from spiritual poverty. He's also symbolic of Jesus' second coming, breaking the chains of poverty and injustice once and for all. Modern-day business owners can follow the example of Boaz by treating their employees and customers with dignity.

Ethical Treatment of Employees and Customers

- Safe working environment
- Fair wages
- Top-quality healthcare to employees and their families— healthcare education onsite and preventative care incentives often lower healthcare costs for employees and employers.
- Flexible work hours
- Education assistance for employees
- Discounts for seniors, students, and customers with low income levels

Financial Independence for Employees and Customers

In the United States we do not owe our debts directly to our places of employment. We may owe debts to banking institutions for houses, cars, education, or healthcare. Unfortunately this load of debt is overwhelming Americans. How can business owners help release their customers and employees from a cycle of debt?

- Encourage incentives and discounts for customers who pay cash. This also helps the bottom line, as employers do not have to pay a percentage of sales to credit card companies.
- Do not conduct business with banking institutions that have predatory lending and interest practices.
- Host a financial planning class on site for employees. <www.crown.org>

Case Study Two: Year of Jubilee Model

If one of your countrymen becomes poor among you and sells himself to you, *do not make him work as a slave.* He is to be treated as a *hired worker* or a temporary resident among you; he is to work for you until the Year of Jubilee. Then *he and his children are to be released*, and he will go back to his own clan and to the property of his forefathers. . . .

Even if he is not redeemed in any of these ways, he and his children are to be released in the Year of Jubilee (*Leviticus 25:39-41, 54, emphasis added*).

Be careful not to harbor this wicked thought: "The seventh year, the year for canceling debts, is near," so that you do not show ill will toward your needy brother and give him nothing. He may then appeal to the LORD against you, and you will be found guilty of sin (*Deuteronomy 15:9*).

"Jubilee" is derived from the Hebrew word *yobel*, signifying a musical blast on a ram's horn.[9] Joyful music was to begin a celebration of freedom for all slaves, prisoners, and debtors. The land and the workers were to rest. Everyone was to enjoy the natural products of the land. Property was the Lord's and restored to the original owners.[10] Some historians believe that the Israelites never fully entered into the celebration—putting down their work, relying on God's provision, and celebrating life and each other.

While we do not observe Jewish rituals, we still ought to strive to practice care for the poorest citizens. How can we translate this into our modern culture to break the cycle of poverty and pain?

Finally Freed

A young boy in India was freed from the dangerous brick kilns. The debt incurred by his great-grandfather caused him to die a slave. The boy's grandfather also died a slave, and the young boy's father almost died paying that original loan.[11] These men faced working conditions beyond our worst imaginings, their employers maiming, burning, cutting, bruising, beating, or starving victims. For better profits? The price of a human life for a cheap ceramic mug?

Contrast this with the previous biblical model. The debtor should be paid as a hired worker. Second, the work would be temporary. Third, the hired hand and his children would be released from the debt.

American companies do not beat, starve, or detain their employees, but those companies can also refuse to do business with companies that do. Will we have the courage to model the glorious compassion of God, or will we, like the Israelites, not join in freedom's celebration?

Consumers, too, can be a part of cutting off the slave owners' business by refusing to be a part of the supply pipeline. Need a place to start? Chain Store Reaction's Web site lists great examples of businesses that monitor those hiring underage workers, setting up preventative measures, designing source labeling, and working with agencies like the Fair Labor Association.

<www.fairlabor.org>

<www.chainstorereaction.com>

Microenterprise

Microfinance provides financial services to the poor as a step toward independence, which can include money transfers, banking, and insurance.[12] Microenterprise consists of small loans made to individuals or groups to start small businesses.[13] Mentorship, financial training—including savings strategies—and job skills may be a part of the microenterprise program.

These loans can be as small as fifty dollars and as large as a few thousand dollars. Loan defaults are very low. When the loan is repaid, the cycle of poverty is broken. The original loan amount is put to good use again as a new loan for another family.

<www.opportunity.org>

<www.endpoverty.org>

Business as Mission (BAM)

Business as Mission has many names such as "Kingdom business," "marketplace missions," and "great commission companies." Business as Mission takes many shapes: microenterprise, ethical business practice, profits for mission work, and church planting. The goal is to make a profit and put that capital to good use.[14] While some businesses may be tempted to promote themselves as a Business as Mission for marketing purposes, those who are really following the guidelines are doing much-needed good in our world.

<www.businessasmissionnetwork.com>

<www.mybusiness-mymission.com>

BUSINESS BENEFIT

There are many positive consequences to living out Kingdom justice at work and in business: a positive work environment, employee retention, good public relations, and the favor and blessing of the Lord. But the best part may be that we are living out what we believe where it is toughest—at work.

Ethics at work doesn't mean slapping a Jesus logo on a brand. We commit to be excellent, the best in our field, the most innovative. And we do this without running others over as we go. The dividing line between secular and sacred blurs as we offer our very best gifts to the Lord. Robert Lupton says,

> Your real estate experience is a gift as precious as gold when presented to the homeless Christ. And with your architectural talents, you may design for him a home. For his broth-

ers and sisters (the least of these), you may design economic innovations to feed and clothe them with dignity. You are invited to bring your most valuable assets—your talent, experience and connections—to create for the Christ a whole new technology of compassion.

Don't reach for your billfold; it is not close enough to your heart. Don't raise your hand to volunteer for another committee in the ecclesiastical bureaucracy; tokenism is an unfit gift. Rather, look within. What invigorates you? What causes you to wake up before dawn with a new idea spinning in your mind? What fuels your imagination, even when you are fatigued? Here is where you will find your most valued treasure. Here is where you will find a gift worthy of your Lord.[15]

REFLECT

1. How is finance a seed?

2. Have you considered stopping to help someone in need during a commute? Have you helped in the past? Why or why not?

3. Do you use your networking skills to help others seeking jobs?

4. How can you harness your business skills to benefit the disadvantaged?

5. What are some unique characteristics of the Boaz and Year of Jubilee models?

6. Is there an area in your business that takes advantage of others or is unethical that needs to change?

7. What "fuels your imagination"? Can you use this to help the disadvantaged?

8. What is the *one* thing you can do to offer better business?

7

Space Invaders

One of the oldest of human needs is having someone to wonder where you are when you don't come home at night.
—Margaret Mead

The click of pool balls, great music, and a basement to ourselves. My group of friends hung out at Todd's house most Friday nights. In my uncertain teen world, it was comforting to know I was always welcome at his house. We took over the basement pool table, TV, and stereo, and we were there till the wee hours. Sometimes the house bulged with thirty kids gathered for a theatre cast party. Todd's parents welcomed everyone; strangers left feeling like family.

On quieter evenings, a few of us sat on the porch swing and contemplated life. Todd's house was a warm, welcoming place where I could be myself. I will always be grateful for that space where I was learning who I was apart from parents, teachers, and authority figures.

In the previous chapters we've looked at ways to live out justice in our daily activities, in the marketplace, and at work. These outlets don't always allow us to come face to face with those who are in need of help. So how to we go about opening our hearts and lives to those who need justice on a personal level—in the same way Todd's parents opened their home to me and my friends when we were teenagers?

THE INVITATION

"Hospitality" is derived from the Latin *hospes*, which is formed from *hostis*, originally meaning "stranger." The Greek word for "hospitality" meant "the love of strangers" and "generosity to guests."[1] In the Greek tradition, hospitality meant shared provision such as food and lodging, protection, and guidance to the next destination.[2] Similar words are "hostel" and "hospital."

I was surprised to learn the original meaning of hospitality. Images of throwing great parties and inviting my friends into my home come to mind when I think of being hospitable. I've never associated it with strangers, mostly just family, friends, and maybe business associates.

I struggle with this concept more than any other when it comes to giving aid to those who need justice. It's hard for me to make space in my life to care for others. Instead, I tend to create a protective insulation to guard my privacy.

I'm an introvert, so I wrap the warm covers of privacy around me. This blanket keeps me warm and protected from the untidy intrusion of others—potential judgment, criticism, and attacks. Unfortunately, that blanket can also insulate me from friendship, love, and growth.

Think of a *hospital*. If an abandoned child was struck down in the street by a speeding car, I would call 911. I would wait for the ambulance and make sure the child received help. I would not leave until I knew the proper procedures were in place for the child's care. Yet when it comes to caring for someone else *in my house*, I look for a way out.

Of course, most of us cannot perform surgery or clean up bloody wounds to promote physical healing, but we can be a welcome refuge from an unfriendly world. We can aid in healing on an emotional and spiritual level. We can provide a refuge.

That's how I remember Todd's house: a peaceful refuge, no questions asked, so that after an emotionally turbulent adolescent day, we could rest and heal.

Inviting others into our lives is often scary, and it usually means making the first move. We can't wait for them to come to us. There's an element of risk in the invitation, but there are also great rewards.

Obedience and the Baby Swing—Sara's Story

When we moved into our new home three years ago, we received a warm reception from our neighbors—well, except for the neighbor directly across the street. She spent a lot of time landscaping, and I often saw her out on a Sunday morning creating beautiful color combinations in her yard. I would wave, but she never responded with even the slightest gesture of notice.

How rude, I thought. *She can't even wave back? Who acts like that?* I dismissed her as a cold person, and she vanished from my thoughts.

Then one afternoon I noticed her teenage daughter was pregnant. I was expecting our second child and lived with a heightened awareness of all things "baby." I sensed the Lord say, "You need to go over there and introduce yourself and offer them anything they need."

I was shocked. *I don't know them. What will they think? They'll think I'm a nosey neighbor butting in; that's what they'll think.* But the quiet glimmer of an idea was solidly forming, and I could not stop thinking of that family.

I asked for guidance from a group I met with every week at church. "I can't just walk over there," I explained. Someone suggested I take cookies as a token of goodwill. Reluctantly, I agreed to approach my neighbor by the end of the week.

I had spoken my plan out loud—a dangerous relief. Now I would really have to go through with it.

The July sun sparkled through our front window on the big day. It was beautiful outside, but I felt sick to my stomach.

All morning I stopped and looked out that window, then sank into the couch. *Is now a good time?* Finally, by the afternoon, I saw a car pull into the driveway. *I just need to go do this.*

I bent over to lace up my daughter's shoes and told her, "We're going over to our neighbor's house. The girl living there is going to have a baby, and we're going to ask her if she needs anything." Chocolate-chip cookies in one hand and Audrey's tiny hand in the other, we walked across the street.

A very pregnant teenager answered the door. I gained confidence from her friendly response. She looked relieved when I offered her the use of my baby items. Her request was simple: "I would just like a swing. Is that something you might have?"

Why had I been so afraid? I felt good as I walked back to my house. It wasn't just about doing a good deed. I'd followed through and done the hard thing even when I was afraid.

The next week I was washing my car and the young woman's mother, who had never even glanced in my direction, walked across the street to meet me. She thanked me for introducing myself to her daughter. She explained that her daughter was isolated from her friends at school. She said that her daughter did need baby items. Other first-time moms could expect a baby shower, but not her daughter. This teenage girl had become the black sheep of her extended family with this early pregnancy.

As we talked, I couldn't believe the change in my neighbor's demeanor.

The door of communication and blessing was open because I obeyed the Lord's tug on my heart. But I hadn't obeyed instantly. I teach my daughter to obey the first time—so I need to be willing to obey my Heavenly Father the first time. Obedience is so sweet. When I moved past judging my "snobby" neighbor, I found a real person with a compelling story.

Jesus as Host

There are many examples in the New Testament of Jesus as the ultimate host. He feeds a crowd of 5,000, turning a few fish and a loaf of bread into a large banquet dinner. He gives good news to the poor, heals the sick, and performs miracles.

My friend Candace has the gift of showing hospitality to large groups. Put her in a room full of women, and she's able to make each one feel welcome and included. She's also blessed with domestic arts skills—organizing, gardening, cooking, and decorating. She's been a professional caterer and cooks for a community center.

Tracey uses her hospitality gift to welcome those who need lodging, and she hosts parties to connect others and support their ministries. She's committed to helping anyone in need.

Some of us—including me—do better one-on-one. I'm so glad Jesus models those intimate hosting moments for us as well. The Jesus of the multitudes called His disciples individually. He didn't audition the crowds in reality television style to find His top twelve. He invited a few men to live everyday life with Him—life victorious and exhilarating; life messy, tired, and dirty; life full of joyous celebration; life suffering—as He faced His own death.

I may not be ready to host a crowd, but I can start with one person. Inviting over one friend who needs encouragement, one person who is down on his or her luck, one person who has been marginalized, or someone who can never repay me is a good start. My hospitality won't make the headlines, especially with my lack of culinary gifts, but it's enough.

Preparations to Host

Jesus' disciples eventually had to put into practice what they had seen Jesus model. Just a week earlier the crowds had shouted, "Hosanna!" Now they screamed, "Crucify!" Last week John enjoyed a Passover celebration feast. This week he watched his best friend die.

Friday was a long day. John was at the foot of the Cross with Mary. Jesus looked down and declared that John was now Mary's son. Mary was John's mother. No extensive instructions.

John was never my favorite disciple. I always felt as if he were the teacher's pet, because he described himself as "the disciple whom Jesus loved." We all knew those kids when we were in school: the blonde girl with braids who knew every answer, the boy who brought the teacher just the right gift on holidays. Jesus had a favorite, and John was it. Right?

What if it's okay that John referred to himself that way? What if it's okay for him to walk in the welcome, the love, the hospitality of Christ? What if Jesus' love for John does not threaten or lessen His love for me? What if Jesus loved all His disciples, but John was wise enough to walk in that love? Jesus didn't own a home, but John made Jesus his home—wherever Jesus happened to be that day—and lived in the light of His welcome.

What if John's best preparation to care for Jesus' mother was not his financial provision or the size of his guest room, but that he walked in the love of Christ and the extension of Christ's love to others? Jesus knew that His mother would be loved.

Sunday Lunch—Lyn's Story

Five years ago my husband started mentoring some young boys once a week. Our church works in partnership with a Christian youth center in a needy area of town. The men from our church fixed up the youth center, and once a week they play basketball and have a Bible study.

My husband, Ken, had a special connection with four of the boys, and that relationship evolved into bringing them to church with us and then to our home for dinner every Sunday. My own children are grown, but they have also been around the table with us.

Some of the boys ride the bus to Ken's work, and he takes them to a game and tries to be a dad to them. We want them to see a larger view of life; most of them know only the three or four blocks right around their homes. Some of them don't have a parent in the home who sets boundaries and cares where they go or what they do.

My husband talks to them about their goals. Jared wants to be a football player. My husband is helping him set small goals like getting the needed physical, keeping his grades up, and being willing to be on the junior high team and attend practices.

It hasn't always been easy. There have been a few times when one boy or another has called and expected us to do something for him or give him money. When that happens, we have to balance what is help against what would not be help. It would be easy to become frustrated and not see where they are coming from. It would be easy to judge them. But when we're all laughing and enjoying each other's company around the table, I know it's all worth it. Lives are being changed—not just theirs but ours too.

I really like the way Lyn made it fun for her guests. The atmosphere is less about décor and more about a warm welcome.

ATMOSPHERE

- Share food responsibilities with others—low stress
- Include activities that appeal to wide interests and ages
- Incorporate games
- Grill out in a park with a playground
- Have a backyard picnic with lawn games
- Share a movie and snacks
- Conduct karaoke night
- Play charades
- Tell stories—real-life or fiction
- Share an activity—cooking, gardening, or something else fun

GUEST LIST

Family

"As we have opportunity, let us do good to all people, especially to those who belong to the family of believers" (Galatians 6:10).

Can you think of someone you can host? In the Old Testament, belonging to the family meant being born into the right tribe. Today we belong to the family of faith by invitation rather than bloodline. We should not leave anyone out or on the sidelines.

Those Who Can't Return the Favor

Jesus said to his host, "When you give a luncheon or dinner, do not invite your friends, your brothers or relatives, or your rich neighbors; if you do, they may invite you back and so you will be repaid. But when you give a banquet, invite the poor, the crippled, the lame, the blind, and you will be blessed. Although they cannot repay you, you will be repaid at the resurrection of the righteous." (*Luke 14:12-14*)

Who can I invite who can't pay me back? Who do I know to invite? Often I associate only with those in my same age group, race, city, social status, and socioeconomic group. I must be willing to befriend a diverse group of people and to extend extra mercy for those in emotional or physical crisis:

- Neighbors
- Coworkers
- Those who are on the front lines of justice ministry
- Church missionaries home on furlough
- Senior citizens—ask them to tell their stories
- International students or college students
- Those grieving the loss of loved ones
- Those with illness or disabilities
- Military families
- Families of prisoners

The writer of the Book of James tells us specifically to look out for "orphans and widows in their distress." Women and children are most vulnerable in crisis situations. In a 2009 report issued in my home state, I learned tht a homeless family is most likely to be a single woman in her thirties with three children.[5]

Vulnerable Women

- Pregnant teens
- Single moms
- Military wives
- Widows
- Divorced women
- Victims of domestic violence, sexual abuse, or sex trafficking

Vulnerable Children

A Piece of Me—Emily's Story

My weekday mornings began with looking into the eyes of twenty-five bright and bubbly kindergarten students. There was a special little boy in my class named Sean. His passion was basketball. He could name the players and teams and recite enough statistics to make your head swim. I could connect math concepts with his love of basketball, and double-digit numbers became players' jersey numbers.

Sean's love of learning and basketball was challenged by his home situation. He was a foster child of an older lady who was overwhelmed and under-resourced to care for him adequately.

I wondered why there aren't more people fostering kids. Why didn't we? The things we do on a daily basis for our own child—reading, playing, and loving her—could change the life of a foster child forever. So I started thinking and praying. My husband was surprised at first, but he soon agreed to proceed.

Foster care certification began with three all-day Saturday training classes. We completed interviews, home inspections, and background checks. Finally we became licensed foster parents. I was really excited and couldn't wait to get the call for our first little visitor. At the same time, I felt weird about being happy. On one hand I couldn't wait to have this baby in my home, but I couldn't imagine the parent's pain of having a child placed in a stranger's home.

One month later I got the call. "We have a six-week-old baby girl who needs a temporary placement. Can you take her?"

"Okay." And a few short hours later we had smiling Sara in our arms. With only the few clothes, diapers, and formula from previous foster parents, I quickly realized she needed more formula and diapers. I would need to get an appointment with the pediatrician.

Lucy, our two-year-old, was in heaven. She brought me the baby's diapers, books, and bottles. Lucy loved playing house with our tiny visitor.

Although I had been in close contact with the case worker and knew of the progress of the relative that would soon be keeping Sara, nothing could prepare me for the reality: "We're coming to pick her up in two days."

Two days! I had just gotten her. I wasn't ready to give her up. Could I already love Sara so much in such a short time?

I tried to prepare Lucy. "Sara is going home to her family on Wednesday. They'll love her and take good care of her." Was I trying to convince Lucy or myself?

Words cannot describe the sadness I felt as I said goodbye, feeling the warmth of her spirit and physical presence leave as I handed her to her new caretaker. I had written a note detailing what she eats, what she likes, her schedule, and the invitation to call me with any questions. I knew I would never see her again, and it felt as if a piece of me trailed out the door as it shut behind little Sara.

I still get choked up when I think about it. But this is what I had trained for, prayed for, and felt called to do. Even though my emotions were upside down, I really did feel peace. I knew that God loves that baby even more than I do. He'll keep her safe, and hopefully she will one day come to know Him as her Heavenly Father.

Our house is busy with Lucy, now four; Skye, age two; and nine-month-old Tyler. We're in the process of adopting Skye, our foster child. I'm so glad that God moved me past the fear of pain to give not only our home and resources but also a piece of me.

Not everyone will be a foster family or adopted family, but we're all instructed to help orphans and widows. The following list is an adaptation of *Ten Ways Every Christian Can Care for the Orphan and Waiting Child,* a resource created by Hope for Orphans®, a ministry of FamilyLife®.[3]

1. Pray

- Put their photograph(s) where you'll remember to pray for them.
- Pray in a group.
  <www.adoptuskids.org>
  <www.rainbowkids.com>

2. Speak Up

- Support foster care through Web site banners, links, bumper stickers, or writing letters to policy-makers.
- Become a court-appointed special advocate for a child in foster care.
  <www.nationalcasa.org>

3. Provide

- Give financial contributions and gifts to orphanages, which could include things like a washing machine, a crib, diapers, and so on.
  <www.helporphans.org>
- Participate in care for orphans overseas.
  <www.gainusa.org> <www.shoesfororphansouls.org>

4. Support

- Mow, baby sit, or organize meals for a week for foster parents. Pray with them, and tell them you appreciate what they do.
- Encourage a family adopting an older child by hosting a shower for them.
- Receive foster care certification to be able to babysit children in foster families.

5. Protect

- Become a "safe family" for families in crisis.
  <www.safe-families.org>
- Become a foster parent or emergency foster parent.
- Help an orphan stay off the streets.
  <www.worldorphans.org>

6. Visit

- Visit orphans overseas.

- Spend time with foster and adoptive families.

7. Give
- Support reputable orphan care organizations on an ongoing basis.
- Contribute generously to an adoptive family to help offset their costs.
  <www.showhope.com> <www.lifesongfororphans.org>

8. Encourage
- Give financial and emotional encouragement through contributions and letters.
  <www.visiontrust.org>
- Tutor or mentor a child—particularly a foster child who will be aging out of the system.

9. Adopt
- Adopt a child in the U.S. or overseas.
  <www.hopefororphans.com>
  <www.christianalliancefororphans.org>

10. Mobilize
- Host guest speakers and adoption-information seminars.
  <www.hopefororphans.com>
  <www.christianalliancefororphans.org>
- Start an adoption network ministry.[4]

Jesus as the Stranger

The last guest on our list would be the stranger—Jesus himself. Matthew records Jesus' strong statement that when we invite a stranger into our homes, we invite Him.[5] The converse is also true. When we don't invite the stranger in, we don't invite Christ. In our vastly different culture, what does that look like today?
- Guests from other towns attending our church events
- Guests arriving in town for a funeral
- Families undergoing medical treatment in our city
- Displaced people from natural disasters— fires, mold toxicity, flooding, tornadoes, earthquakes, and so on

PAY-OFF

There are bound to be awkward moments when we reach out in the ways described.

During my college internship, I lived in a house with a group of college kids and a homeless man. When we left for work, we all wondered what Jim would do while we were gone. We hadn't thought that far ahead when we invited him to move in.

It was awkward when I lent my husband's fleece jacket to a needy kid and was irritated when it wasn't returned. I probably should have just given it to him in the first place.

We can't welcome the whole world into our living rooms. But we can start by welcoming a few. I pray about which opportunities I can say yes to and let myself be okay with what I'm unable to do. I let go of past mistakes, the times I should have said yes. I remember how I felt when others took the time to invite me in.

THE TABLE

King David had returned from battle, victoriously defeating his enemies. He was reigning over a now-peaceful Israel and decided to show kindness to any relatives of his recently deceased best friend, Jonathan. A servant mentioned that a crippled son of Jonathan's was living.

Jonathan's son had reason to be afraid. His father was Jonathan, but his grandfather was Saul, David's enemy. But David reassured him of his safety. He restored the land of King Saul, gave servants to work the land, and promised him a place at the king's table. David could have provided for this cripple from a distance. The beauty is that when David offered the young man a place at the table, he offered friendship and relationship.

Jesus, like David, offers us a place at His table. What cost David land and possessions cost Christ His life—so that we would have communion with Him. Not just redemption but a relationship is offered. We who are crippled spiritually have a place to rest, eat, and heal.

Once I've enjoyed the comforts of such a host, can I refuse hospitality to those around me? I can't let the trivial costs of food, time, and energy be my excuse any longer when I'm physically and spiritually renewed by such a gracious host.

REFLECT

1. Who has offered you great hospitality? What made it so memorable?

2. Are you comfortable hosting others? Why or why not?

3. Did you learn something new in any of these stages of welcome? If so, what?
    Invitation
    Preparation
    Atmosphere
    Guest List
    The Table (mercy)

4. How is Christ our host? How is He our guest?

5. What is the *one* thing you can do to offer better hospitality?

8

AWAY FROM HOME

Before many days had passed I had found out my poor,
who, I thought, must be somewhere.[1]
—George MacDonald

One warm summer during my grade school years I enrolled in a reading program at the local library. I loved reading, but not the books on the required list. And it was summer after all. I preferred the *Choose Your Own Adventure Books*. These books placed me as the main character with decisions to make like "If you narrowly escaped and hitched a ride home with the cowboys, turn to page 36," or "If you got captured by the bank robbers, turn to page 40."

They were fun for a while. But I often didn't like a certain ending. I figured that if I was in charge of this story, I should get the ending I liked. I found a way to achieve this by mapping out a couple different pathways through different endings until I arrived at the best choice. But once this started, a strange thing happened: I lost interest in the books. The adventure and surprise ending vanished.

Helping others at home, the marketplace, and business are great ways to serve. But there's something special about surprise endings, about leaving my comfortable surroundings and the people who are familiar to me. The endings don't always turn out the way I envision, but I learn, grow, and have the most fun.

Sometimes I forget to bring along a sense of adventure and panic as I try to map out the bad things that might happen, just as I did with the adventure books. "If I serve here, then I might not have time to get my work done, and my schedule will fall apart" or "If I help someone who's sick, then I might get sick, too, and lose too much time." Planning is good. Over-thinking is not.

A grand adventure calls. What page will you turn to?

A Different Kind of Adventure Hero

We like our adventure heroes to be strong, brave, brilliant, and decisive. In literature and film, we see the icons of kings, knights, generals, presidents, and even the everyman underdogs shine brightly through their characters. They forge their own paths and overcome all obstacles.

But Christians see our true hero, Jesus, doing things a little differently. He often said He followed directions from God. Hmmm, a hero taking orders? Seems strange. But as a result, Jesus' adventures took Him to many different places, including a wedding and a wilderness, a mountaintop and a tomb.

Jesus' travels also took Him to people—all kinds of people. From the very first years of life He encountered shepherds, kings, angels, priests, and the poor. Later He would encounter Pharisees, prostitutes, rulers, generals, and tax collectors. But He spent most of His time around the marginalized of society—an unlikely choice in His adventure story.

Our Adventures

Toward the end of our adventure hero's life, He made some predictions about His return. What adventures would His followers experience before He comes back?

> When the Son of Man comes in his glory, and all the angels with him, he will sit on his throne in heavenly glory. All the nations will be gathered before him, and he will separate the people one from another as a shepherd separates the sheep from the goats. He will put the sheep on his right and the goats on his left.

Then the King will say to those on his right, "Come, you who are blessed by my Father; take your inheritance, the kingdom prepared for you since the creation of the world. For I was hungry and you gave me something to eat, I was thirsty and you gave me something to drink, I was a stranger and you invited me in, I needed clothes and you clothed me, I was sick and you looked after me, I was in prison and you came to visit me."

Then the righteous will answer him, "Lord, when did we see you hungry and feed you, or thirsty and give you something to drink? When did we see you a stranger and invite you in, or needing clothes and clothe you? When did we see you sick or in prison and go to visit you?"

The King will reply, "I tell you the truth, whatever you did for one of the least of these brothers of mine, you did for me" (*Matthew 25:31-40*).

Our returned hero will know that we're His because we're continuing the work He started before He left. His adventures must become ours. This is not an all-inclusive list of where to help, but these six categories are a good place to start: hunger, thirst, shelter, clothing, sickness, and visits.

Where do you go when you leave home to help others? The following are a few ideas.

Hunger

- Soup banks
- Food pantries
- Food reclamation
- Food banks
- Shelters
- City missions
- Developing countries

Thirst

- Volunteer to assemble, package, and test water treatment systems.

- Take a trip and give clean water (well-drilling, pump repair, or hygiene education).
  <www.water.cc>

Shelter

- Rebuild homes following tsunamis, hurricanes, earthquakes.
  <www.shelterforlife.org>
- Build houses.
  <www.amor.org>
- Build orphanages.
- Adopt-a-block for neighborhood restoration.
- Provide housing materials and repairs.
  <www.christianapp.org>
- Share your home.
  <www.nationalsharedhousing.org>
- Volunteer at a shelter.

Clothing

- Organize a baby shower to provide clothes and infant items to low income moms.
- Teach others how to sew.
  <www.opendoorsusa.org>

Sickness

SickNet. Start a local SickNet, a group that volunteers on a rotating basis to help in emergency situations. When someone calls in with a need, the volunteers bring a meal or offer to do light cleaning or errands. The volunteers could be a neighborhood or church group.[2]

Visits

- Share music, live or recorded.
- Complete home projects: spring plantings, leaf-raking, putting up Christmas lights.
- Visit those with AIDS or cancer.

Errands

- Transport to doctor's appointments.
- Take to church or community events.
- Drive the injured, recuperating, or disabled to work if they can't drive themselves.
- Deliver groceries or other necessary items.

Gifts

- Drop off flowers or cards.
- Provide movies or books.
- Plan holiday surprises.

Connections

- Organize family and friends to send well wishes.
- Help them update blogs or Web sites to keep family and friends aware of progress.
  <www.caringbridge.org>

Sick Children

- Engage in activities with coloring books, small toys, or games.
- Take your children to visit, and share their art work with sick kids.
  <www.artistshelpingchildren.org>
- Take food to families with sick children.

Global Illness

- Package medicines that will go overseas.
  <www.map.org>
- Visit the sick overseas.
- Provide a "lab in a suitcase" for a doctor overseas.
  <www.internationalaid.org>
- Support disease prevention by providing simple items such as mosquito netting for malaria.
  <www.compassion.com>

THE IMPRISONED

Prisoners and Their Families

- Visit them.
- Lead a prison Bible study.
- Mentor a prisoner.
- Tutor prisoners or their children.
- Teach job skills.
- Distribute Bibles.
- Write letters to them.
- Provide meeting space for videophone calls from families to inmates.
- Broadcast Sunday sermons to inmates and families.
- Provide post-release counseling.
  <www.goodnewsjail.org>
  <www.pfm.org>

The Persecuted Church

- Write encouraging letters to religious prisoners and their families.
  <www.prisoneralert.com>
  <www.persecution.com>
- Sign and circulate petitions to governments unjustly holding Christians.
  <www.persecution.org/suffering/petitions.php>
- Meet with others in your area working to end persecution.
  <www.vommeetings.com>
- Visit the persecuted—pray with them; deliver Bibles, medicine, and material support.
  <www.christianfreedom.org>
- Visit the persecuted—complete socioeconomic projects, deliver Bibles, conduct literacy training.
  <www.opendoors.org>

Shut Down Slavery

I hit me hard to see that it was happening where I live. I opened a map of the United States on my computer, clicked on my state, and there was a report of slavery in my city. A woman was lured with a babysitting job and held captive for a week, along with two other girls, in a sex-trafficking operation.[3]
<www.slaverymap.org>

Many of us know the signs to watch for to help keep each other safe from drunk drivers, neighborhood crime, or domestic violence. We know to call 911 and get help immediately. But few of us know to watch for signs of slavery and human trafficking. The United States Department of Health and Human Services' Web site gives ways to spot and report these practices.[4]

What?
Human trafficking is a modern-day form of slavery.
Victims of human trafficking are subjected to force, fraud, or coercion for the purpose of sexual exploitation or forced labor.

Who?
Young children, teenagers, men, and women.
More than half of the 600,000 to 800,000 trafficked each year are children.

Where?
- Commercial sex
- Domestic servitude (servants)
- Sweatshop factories
- Construction
- Farming or landscaping
- Fisheries
- Hotel or tourist industries
- Panhandling
- Janitorial services
- Restaurant services

<www.acf.hhs.gov/trafficking>
<www.humantrafficking.org>

Common Signs of Trafficked Person
• Fearful
• No recognition of home or work address
• Can't take breaks or go out alone at work
• Lack of social integration
• Signs of physical abuse or malnutrition
• Accompanied by overprotective guardian or employer

To Report
Call the National Human Trafficking Resource Center:
888-3737-888 (or 911 in an emergency)
(See the Appendix for more details on spotting trafficking.)

I was surprised to learn that some victims work in beauty sa-lons, restaurants, or in hotels. We can educate ourselves to look out for those in distress.

There are many more people groups that still need justice. The table in chapter one lists more groups. Also the Appendix shows justice needs and reputable organizations ready to partner with you to make a difference. Anyone who is marginalized needs our help.

ANY CAUSE

Here are some other great ways to help the cause of your choice.

Awareness
• Wear a T-shirt supporting a cause.
  <www.abort73.com>
• Display bumper stickers or logos.
• Utilize social networking or Web site logos or links to char-ity.
• Attend a rally.
• Upload a photo.

- Protest or freeze in silence. Groups of people go to a public place and stand silently, sometimes with T-shirts or signs to draw attention to a cause.
- Communicate messages with the arts.
- E-mail political leaders.
- Write a blog or a letter to the editor.

Fundraising
- Walk or run for a fundraising event.
- Organize a fundraising event.
- Plan a neighborhood block party.
- Attend a concert benefit.
- Invite your large group to collect loose dollars and change.
- Auction items or services.

WHO'S GOING WITH ME?

Many volunteers have one thing in common: feelings of guilt for leaving family or friends to go serve. We need to find a way to include these important people in our adventures. It's good for us to do things together. There is an energy and excitement in a group that can't be recreated alone. I really don't like physical exercise, but even that's more fun when I take a class. The group's energy and excitement are contagious. We learn differently in a group. The group processes volunteering together. This allows for deeper thinking and spiritual growth.

Adventure with Family

The Real Story—Melinda's Story

I wasn't so sure about taking my first real overseas mission trip with my daughter. Kelly had recently completed her junior year of high school. It was already a struggle to know how to relate to her world at home and to prepare for the transition of releasing her into her college years. How was our relationship going to be tested on foreign soil, minus the insulation and comforts of home?

On the Midday Moms on a Mission trip, those fears were soon put to rest as we visited Guatemalan orphanages, played games with children, shared the gospel, and provided school supplies we had collected from home.

To be honest, there were a few tense mom-daughter moments with some of the duos on the trip, but overall it was a wonderful bonding time. Moms and daughters came together on equal ground—learning new things together in a third-world environment—and relied on each other to get through the days in unique ways. The daughters also got to process the trip in their peer group in their own teen language. They continued those conversations with old friends at home.

The trip was life-changing for my daughter, Kelly. Learning a foreign language is difficult. She was slugging through Spanish before. But she came back with a renewed excitement to see how God could use her growing knowledge of a second language. It really did apply to her life! This trip impacted the direction of her life as Kelly continues to grow a passion for international work.

It impacted me as well. Shopping for the first time was hard. How do you process what you need at the store after being around those who don't have clothes or closets and whose homes are small patchwork pieces of cinder blocks?

How do I take what I learned and let it sink into the crevices of my heart? There's no good answer to that question. I just listen differently now. From the needs in my own community represented by the beggar at the train station to women's pain that I hear in my daily work to a church friend broken by divorce—I withhold judgment and listen with an ear tuned to the music of compassion.
<www.middayconnection.org>

Adventure with Friends

Cross Training—Fourteen-Year-Old Katie's Story

I enjoy athletics, specifically participating in the girls' cross country and track teams. I have many friends on the teams, and we have so much fun. I wanted to do a service event that would involve our whole team, so we unloaded lots of boxes and items off a large truck at our local fairgrounds for a charity's "Christmas Give-Away." It was so cold! All of us and our parents got a day's worth of work done in two hours. Twenty thousand families who had pre-registered had the chance to give their kids a better Christmas with food, toys, gifts, clothes, and Christmas trees. Mom said the other parents were surprised to see the needs in our own neighborhood.

My friends and I have made volunteering a part of our hang-out time, and I take them with me to do childcare for a local clinic. We watch children while their parents get medical attention. Last Saturday a few friends came for the first time. I could tell they were really uncomfortable in a strange part of town and new surroundings. It was really neat to see my friends open up and start having fun as we jumped rope and played sharks and minnows and freeze tag.

These children long for positive attention and really enjoy the simplest games or the toys they receive. It makes me grateful to have the things I have, such as a good breakfast or a doctor when I need one.

It may sound selfish, but I almost get more out of it than the people I am helping. It has changed me, because I know that serving is what I'm good at. I really encourage kids my age to get involved and take their friends with them. It's so fun to share that part of your life with friends.

I love the fact that Katie did not wait until she was older to get involved and that her parents allow her the freedom to choose her adventure. Her education is not just what she learns at school but also what she's learning in life.

The true end of education is not only to make the young learned,
But to make them love learning,
Not only to make them industrious,
But to make them love industry,
Not only to make them virtuous,
But to make them love virtue . . .

Not only to make them just,
But to make them hunger and thirst after justice.

—John Ruskin

Adventure with a Group

Able to Connect—Jill's Story

When I was growing up I wondered, *Why was I born into a region of prosperity? Why do other people, just by virtue of where they live, suffer?* Those thoughts come back to me now as I recall my fifteen years of involvement with Mission to Ukraine.

Our purpose is to bring people to Christ through humanitarian aid. Why the Ukraine—it's Europe, right? Isn't all the poverty in Africa?

Ukraine has much poverty, and very few have access to adequate resources. They're much poorer than even the poorest Americans. We connect with a lot of their orphans and orphanages. Most leave the orphanages by the age of fifteen or sixteen. Seventy percent of once-orphaned girls end up in prostitution, while twenty-five percent of boys are dead by the age of twenty. The average lifespan for orphans is thirty years. Clearly, reaching out to orphans early is key.

It's even worse for the disabled orphans, as they're marginalized by society. Many are locked away and have never been outside. Our main partner orphanage is cared for by a kind headmaster who welcomes our assistance. Sadly, many orphanages don't want our help, because it's easier to continue the neglect.

We partnered with my home church's Special Friends Sunday School class of disabled children. They, along with other volunteers, packed toys, socks, scarves, hats, gloves, mittens, and underwear into shoe bags. A handwritten note was added to each one with a photo of the person packing the items. Disabled children on both sides of the world were making a connection.

The Ukrainian leader wrote about how excited the children were and how quickly they opened the bags. They had their first real Christmas. They touched warm scarves for the first time. They played with their first toys and stuffed animals.

I wish I could show you before-and-after photos of the children. Non-responsive children who were barely crawling are now walking, smiling, and getting necessary therapy through activities our staff provides.

As I go about my work with Mission to Ukraine, I don't want to get in the way by thinking that I do this. God does the work and simply allows me to participate. I work every day to better convey to citizens in the United Stats that we must care, because what happens to them involves us as well. <www.missiontoukraine.org>

All three of these women are of a different age and life stage, but all three found ways to serve with family, friends, and groups. They have something in common—joy. In each interview, passion and excitement for life were contagious as I heard how God used each woman's individual interests and skills to meet needs in the world. They're saying yes to the adventure.

If there were no restraints on time, money, resources, or energy, what would you love to do with your friends? Where would you like to go with your family? Can you take your *one* thing and serve as a group? What information or training might you need? Pray for direction as to where you should go, and ask God, who owns all resources and time, for the courage to go.

The adventure always leads to life—real life.

"I came so they can have real and eternal life, more and better life than they ever dreamed" (John 10:10, TM).

That life dripped off the dew in the first garden and swirled in the storm that rocked Noah's ark. The energy split a sea in half—a path of freedom for God's people—and established a nation ruled by God. That spark lit a blaze of battles and kingdoms to flicker faintly through the darkness of the prophets. The song began faintly in the womb of a teenage girl and shouted forth "Hosanna!" in Jerusalem. The force ripped the sky apart as Jesus suffered on the Cross and rolled back a large stone on Resurrection day.

The adventure did not stop between Bible times and today. Centuries of believers have had real life drip, split, spark, and blaze a journey. Early Christians hid in catacombs to pray. Men and women smuggled the Bible into the hands of scribes so we could have it in our own language. Reformation and revivals broke forth in Europe. In the last century human rights reform and humanitarian aid have begun to spread globally, and the gospel goes out to the far ends of the earth today.

The epic journey is not complete.

It is our turn and our story.

Will we step into the adventure?

Reflect

1. What have your adventures been like serving away from home? Was it a good experience? Why or why not? What did you learn?

2. Why did Christ spend most of His time with those who were marginalized?

3. Why does He instruct us to interact with those who are marginalized?

4. Have you served with family, friends, or other group? If so, did that have any impact on your motivation to continue?

5. Which idea resonated most with you from each of these sections?
   Hunger
   Thirst
   Shelter
   Clothing
   Sickness
   The Imprisoned
   Any Cause

6. Pick *one* focus area from the list above.

Part III
Reality Check

REAL MESS, REAL REWARDS

The best way out is always through.
—Robert Frost

For two summers Aaron and I worked a booth at music festivals for Compassion International to gain sponsorships for kids in developing countries. What could be easier? Work the table. Answer questions. Influence people to sponsor children. Camp out for the weekend at the festival. What started out innocently turned into hilarity.

During the first year we pitched our tent next to some college kids we befriended. After a long June day of blistering heat and sunburned hands and feet, we finally fell asleep around 2 A.M. to the chatter and giggles of our neighbors. Soon after, a gentle rain began to fall, thunder rumbling in the distance. Around 3 A.M. we were jolted awake by a blinding flash of lightning and a loud clap of thunder. I literally felt the electric heat surge through us. We could hear screaming and more chatter from across the campground as a number of folks made a run for their cars. Then we heard the sirens of an ambulance coming to transport an injured camper to the hospital. Sunrise came way too soon that morning, and we were up again to work the Compassion booth.

There were supposed to be shower facilities onsite, but no such luck, and after three days we were plastered with dirt. Despite the craziness, more than a hundred kids were sponsored, and all we could do was look at each other and laugh. We couldn't take ourselves seriously if we tried.

The following year I brought disposable ponchos to lure people to the table. We marked the ponchos to advertise Compassion International and prayed for rain. I guess it worked too well. We ran out of ponchos in ten minutes and ended up sloshing through mud to keep our tiny tent from flying away in the storm.

That seemed to be the pattern throughout my advocacy work: presentation mistakes, unusable technology, losing my way, and receiving my only traffic violations on the way to Compassion events. I didn't know whether to laugh or cry. Sometimes I did both.

One of every three volunteers will discontinue his or her service by the next year.[1] The dropout rate may be even higher for those who work to end injustice.

Annoyances, inconveniences, and relationship conflicts are leading causes for dropping volunteer work. As Aaron and I battled through them all, I was tempted to believe the lie that my life was better before.

To avoid dissatisfaction and burnout, it's helpful to know as much as possible about the organization for which you intend to volunteer. This helps the organization and you.

Questions to ask:

- What is the mission statement of this organization?
- Does it present a clear gospel message as well as service to those who need justice?
- Does it promote long-term change as well as temporary relief?
- What kind of training will I receive?
- What will be my job description, responsibilities, and time commitment?
- Can I volunteer with family or friends to make it a richer experience?
- Does the charity have self-evaluation processes in place for ongoing improvements? Can the volunteers contribute feedback in this process?

Once you've done your homework and feel that this is the place for you, you'll want to make the commitment to keep going even when you're feeling stretched.

COMMIT WHEN YOU'RE STRETCHED

Me, a Leader?—Teresa's Story

Along with a group of friends, my children and I began serving by helping with an evening meal at a mission. The kids enjoyed it, and it helped them learn to appreciate ordinary things—like food and a home. My son stationed himself in the dishroom where he could talk to men as they returned their trays. My daughter and I helped in the main dining room with dessert. Some of our friends felt uncomfortable with the men we were serving, because they thought they had little in common, but we enjoyed serving together as a group, and my family and I were hooked.

It's easy to see the face of Christ in the poor—these men who have few material possessions often have strong faith. They are willing to ask for help, request prayers, and share their stories, even dark details of addictions, giving God the glory for their restored lives.

A few years later I went on a trip to Toronto with a church group. Most mission trips focus on *doing*: building houses, running children's programs, feeding the hungry. This was not a go-to-*do* trip—it was a go-to-*be* trip. The purpose was to see Christ in a broken world, to see the hurting people as He sees them. It was life-changing.

During a time of reflection, I waited to hear from God about how to apply what I had learned through this experience. I felt Him urging me to take a step to begin to lead others. I immediately started backpedaling in my mind. *I'm not comfortable with that. I'm happy where I am. Can I do something else?*

Not long after that, somebody at the men's mission approached me about leading groups of new volunteers to teach them how serve during the evening dinner time. I had the courage from the Lord to say yes. I'm still not a big fan of that word—"lead." God leads. I just guide or facilitate, taking care of the logistical stuff.

Since that time, I've continued to allow God to stretch me. I've now guided two teams back to Toronto and will facilitate a mission trip to New York. I'm more aware of the opportunities God places in my life, and I'm blessed beyond measure to go where He sends me.

COMMIT WHEN YOU'RE MISUNDERSTOOD

I have a great time getting sponsors for kids in other countries. I love connecting kids in developing countries with families in the United States. I'm not the one on the front lines working in the heat, the mud, and disease. But I do find myself getting a different kind of compassion fatigue.

I feel the undercurrent of unkind words about my volunteer work from those who misunderstand, either from those I'm trying to persuade to participate in child sponsorship or others who just think this is all pretty weird.

I realized the irony one day while speaking with friends who also work to end poverty. They commiserated with me about similar frustrations. I think it took hearing someone else verbalize what I had been thinking for me to clearly hear my own negative attitude. The whole point to my advocacy work was mercy, yet I was being anything but merciful in my rationalizations.

It's often hardest to be kind to those who are around us in everyday life. It may be easier to have empathy for a starving child around the globe than the person next to me who misunderstands my heart. Real mercy should extend to both. True compassion must include those around us, not just those with whom we agree or who truly understand what we are trying to do. How grateful I am for those gracious people in my life who put up with my shortcomings, character flaws, and the underdeveloped areas of my spiritual life! Shouldn't I be kind when I feel belittled?

COMMIT WHEN YOU FEEL MISTREATED

If we get past crazy circumstances, internal struggles, and misunderstandings, at least we can rely on those we help to be kind and appreciative. Right?

Stolen Watch—Regina's Story

In 1998 I led a group from my church in North Carolina on a mission trip to Haiti. On that trip I prepared to spend a day with my sponsored child, Natasha, along with other Compassion sponsors from my church who were meeting their sponsored children. I had visions of a most glorious day—a blessed, made-in-heaven type of day.

But when I met her, the day felt more like hell than heaven. It was extremely hot, and we were crowded into a stuffy room that had no air-conditioning. I was dehydrated and feeling weak.

Meeting Natasha was awkward. She didn't seem overjoyed to see me, as I had imagined she would. She was shy, very reserved, avoided making eye contact for the longest time, and even seemed a little unfriendly.

We didn't share a common language—Natasha spoke Creole, and I spoke English—but it took no time at all for me to realize she was trying to get me to understand that she wanted my watch. She wanted my watch a lot more than she wanted the Creole Bible with its pretty, flowered carry-case that I had brought her as a gift. So I gave her my watch and felt hurt, used, and exploited.

But God wouldn't let me wallow in self-pity. He used a few well-timed observations from a friend on the trip to shake me out of my pity party. My friend Karen commented on how unusually underdeveloped and emotionally immature Natasha seemed to be for her age—probably indicating long-term malnutrition when she was very young and ongoing malnutrition now that she was fifteen.

The thought of the tremendous suffering my little girl had most likely experienced made the surrender of my two-year-old Timex sports watch seem like such an insignificant thing.

Through this experience with my watch, God showed me how selfish my expectations for Natasha had been. I had gone to Haiti wanting to experience her love for me, wanting to see how grateful she was for what I had been doing for her, wanting her to be who and how I wanted her to be—not who she actually was.

God showed me that loving others is messy and that loving the poor can be *very* messy. He showed me that we must love the poor not because we want to be loved back or shown gratitude. We must love the least of these not because we think it will make us feel good.

We must love them whether or not they're nice people or respond the way we hope they will, whether or not they're grateful, and whether or not they take advantage of us. We must love them because Jesus loves them—and because Jesus loved us while we were still sinners, and He died for us all.

God used Natasha in a supernatural, wonderfully sacremental way in my life in spite of her fallen nature—and in spite of my fallen nature. And he can do the same thing in your life. Don't let your fears keep you from the wonderful, risky adventure of letting your heart be broken.[2]

No one volunteers to be mistreated, but those things happen. Think of your past—the things that have broken you, the things that have caused you pain—and then add the pressures of poverty or injustice on top of that. Often recipients of our help may feel distrust, entitlement, or resentment toward us. But in every moment of heartache in relationships we find redemption, restoration, and growth right along with the brokenness.

Commit When It's Messy

Pick a Corner—Lauren's Story

A few years ago our church announced the grand opening of its new community center and issued an invitation for a tour and reception. It may sound silly, but the promise of cake won me over. My husband and I were impressed with the facilities and programs and asked the director about his future plans for the center. He mentioned that the hope was to start a medical clinic. With only one doctor on board and so much to do, it seemed a far-off dream. My husband, a pharmacist, and I, a nurse, had been on a medical ministry team at church. It was the one time I felt God gently push me forward, and before I knew it, "Let me contact some people" flew out of my mouth.

In six months we had the clinic open with a lab, a fully stocked pharmacy, a prestigious medical director who had worked for the Veterans Administration, and a policy book that could rival any hospital's. Anyone in the medical profession could tell you that an accomplishment of this magnitude in such a short time frame was something of a miracle.

Our volunteers have learned some hard lessons in tough love. Not long after the clinic was opened, we realized a patient was having blood drawn every week. We finally realized she was just using the clinic to check her cholesterol. She was also leaving with a large supply of our medications—about four hundred pills in a month—and handing them out to family and friends. We finally had to enforce our regulations, which meant filing the paperwork and following our procedures, or no more service. It was difficult but necessary for us to use our resources in the best way.

You can't let the long hours and few instances of misconduct by patients overshadow the importance of your work. It's often the simple things, like taking someone's blood pressure or walking him or her through the early diagnosis of diabetes, that can truly change a life and calm real fears.

A grandmother brought in an infant with an ear infection and a temperature of 102 degrees. Less than two dollar's worth of antibiotics and Tylenol did the trick. The woman was so grateful, and I knew we were doing vital work.

Our clinic is run with the utmost professional care, labs, medications, and follow-up with patients. Just because the patients are poor doesn't mean they don't deserve the best care. If we don't help them, who will?

Before volunteering at this clinic, I had been a surgical nurse for sixteen years. One surgery lasted sixteen hours. When the patient and the doctors left the room, it looked like a war zone. We were exhausted and still had to clean up before we could leave. I turned to the other nurse and said, "I don't know where to start." She replied, "Pick a corner and work your way out."

That's how I view helping the needy. We see the war zone of hunger, AIDS, and other tragedies, and we sometimes don't know where to start. But making a difference in one person's life is huge. Pick one thing and try it. Find a small corner and work your way out.

Commit When It's Not Safe

We've seen perseverance through circumstances, internal struggles, misunderstandings, and mistreatment by those we try to help. Some volunteers feel they could get past all those issues if they felt they could serve and stay out of physical danger.

A decade ago, I traded in my preppy college dorm for the gorgeous backdrop of the Rocky Mountains. Our daytime work was in the inner city with the homeless, the hungry, and at-risk children. Each group of us had different ministry centers during the work week and rode public transportation to get there.

On Saturday mornings we all joined together to present a kids' morning puppet show and snacks in the park. Then later in the morning we worked a food relief line in a parking lot.

Tired and grumpy from the long week, we found Saturday was always the hardest day for us. We were accustomed to thinking of Saturday as *ours*—a free day. But now Saturdays were the hardest days due to the intense face-to-face interaction with the needy who would be coming through the food relief line.

There were young families, pregnant moms with small children, thankful for the help. Many were older homeless men, often injured or high. The body odor was overwhelmingly magnified by the intensity of the heat rising up from the black pavement where we stood.

Once in a while there were inappropriate advances. We would give them the food with a smile and keep the line going. The members of our group watched out for each other. Some of the guys stood on the corner, Bibles open, engaging the men in conversations about Christ. Some of us who knew Spanish were engaged with a couple of Latino children.

One morning I was stung by a bee as we were packing up from the park to leave for the food line. We volunteers had strict instructions not to separate ourselves from the group because of safety issues. Because of my severe allergy to bee stings, I panicked and hurried off to a restroom. I wasn't sure anyone in our group had a car; most of us used public transportation. Even if someone had a car, where was the nearest hospital?

When I came out of the bathroom to look for help, two men approached me. They made inappropriate advances, and I was cornered. I knew better than to have let myself get into that situation! In tears I looked up to see our group leader and another girl, and the two men left. We were able to locate a car and get to a first aid clinic.

I was fortunate. It could have turned out badly. What if it had gone the other way? Would it have been worth it to serve in that place? My story does not compare to those of many who have encountered danger and had an unhappy outcome. There's a rich history of believers who ran toward danger, refusing to deny Christ, and who have faced torture, risking illness and disease, to take the gospel to remote areas. Many of those died, living their faith.

It would have been easier to stay home—no bee stings, no advances from strange men, no public transportation, no delayed flights, no unfamiliar food, no missing my friend's funeral, and no spending a summer away from home.

But choosing safety would have been very costly. If I hadn't gone on that trip I would not have

- learned to get along with students from all races and socioeconomic backgrounds from across the country.
- learned how to lead a child to Christ.
- learned to push through physical obstacles—heat, sweat, exhaustion—to the end.
- learned to depend on Christ for strength to be gracious in hard circumstances.
- experienced life-changing worship at a truly diverse church.
- planned worship time for the first time for kids and gained valuable experience in my field of study—music education.

I'm so grateful that I didn't go with rest of my friends on a beach trip. God was calling me to something different. I almost didn't go—but I'm not sure it would have been safer to stay home.

COMMIT WHEN YOU WANT TO QUIT

All the times we are in danger, stretched, misunderstood, mistreated, or misused may leave us thinking there's only one thing to do—just quit. It would be so much easier. What makes someone stay? Why would anyone keep going?

The Most Important Thing—Brenda's Story

I still have the picture of my son Dylan hugging his friend Brayan in Ecuador. The love in that embrace knew no bounds. Now, as a proud mom of teens volunteering to end child poverty, I look back to see that those times we gave ourselves away were the threads that connected the hearts of our family.

One would think life might get less hectic as my oldest daughter headed off to college, but it only sped up. I struggled with health difficulties, increased work load, and felt torn between my leadership position in volunteer work and home. I felt like a fraud. *These other volunteers are doing so well and have such a great ministry. What am I doing?*

I announced to my family that I was quitting. My son insisted, "Mom, you can't. This is the most important thing you do." That statement was life-changing.

As a mom, you wonder, *Which part of what I'm trying to teach them will stick? What will they remember?* I was so proud that he learned that justice work is important enough to keep going.

I would like to say that after that moment, service was easy. But it continued to be a struggle to find my missing joy. How could I do a good job of inspiring others when I was doing a lousy job of inspiring my own family? This inner conflict continued into the next year.

After not being able to reconcile service with my real life, I decided I had no other choice but to step down. I sat with my supervisor, Rick, to brainstorm ideas for my replacement. He listened patiently and then gently probed, "Where is your heart? Is this still what you want to do?" In my heart I cried out *Yes! I love this!* Then I remembered hitting all those brick walls. How could I keep giving when I felt done?

He responded, "I'll take what you can give, and we'll figure out the rest." We delegated some of my responsibilities to other team members, not only lightening my load but also giving them a greater sense of leadership. Rick found a way to work out the logistics. He, like Christ, is asking all of us, "Where are your hearts? What do you treasure?"

1 John 3:16 says, "This is how we know what love is: Jesus Christ laid down his life for us. And we ought to lay down our lives for our brothers." That phrase echoed through my being. "Lay down your life." I'm willing to give what I have left, my leftovers, but He calls me to something different. Inconvenience, stress, or time given is just my small way to give up my life.

When I get past discouragement, I remember that I've seen God come through in amazing ways for the poor. That same God provides in amazing ways for me to continue this work.

I couldn't do this without the support of my family who has "vacationed" with me very creatively in random parts of the country. We have canoed, hiked, swum, and gone sightseeing around my conference schedules. My husband has loaded up the van, carried boxes, signed new sponsors, and fired up the grill for Compassion events. My family has been there every step of the way, as this is not just an activity but a way of life in service that has brought us closer together.

No matter what, we aren't going to quit.

<www.compassion.com>

Commit to Hold on to Jesus

"The impact God has planned for us does not occur when we're pursuing impact—it occurs when we're pursuing God" (Phil Vischer, creator of *Veggie Tales*).

Pursing impact or God? I often move my laser beam focus off Him and onto what I'm doing *for* Him.

There are days when I honestly wonder, *What am I doing? I'm so tired.* But I know that if I put my hope in Him, He'll restore my strength.[3] God does not grow tired and weary but has an endless supply of energy, creativity, and life ready for me when I ask Him.

Commit Till the End

I want to finish what I started in this justice journey. I don't want to leave this important work like so many half-completed projects strewn about the house.

There is a beautiful scene in John Bunyan's *The Pilgrim's Progress* that my mind returns to often.

Pilgrim sees the beautiful palace and longs to rest there. He enters a narrow passage and sees two lions, which he had been warned about by the characters Mistrust and Timorous. Pilgrim stops, because he doesn't want to die. Then Watchful, the porter at the palace, shouts out to Pilgrim that the lions are chained and that he should keep in the middle of the path. Pilgrim shakes in his fear as he walks toward the palace. The lions roar but do not harm him.[4]

Inconvenience, misunderstanding, mistreatment, fear, and exhaustion are lions that roar loudly.

Have you seen them lately?

Felt the steel of their gaze?

The strength of their lunge?

The heat of their breath?

The noise of their roar?

Keep on, friend—the lions are chained.

REFLECT

1. What kind of mess have you experienced in serving? Was it comical or tearful?

2. What kind of reward have you experienced in serving? Was it worth the effort?

3. Which broken piece is most discouraging?

4. What restored piece is most encouraging?

5. Which "commit" section can you most identify with?
   Inconvenienced
   Stretched
   Exhausted
   Mistreated
   Safety compromised

6. Are you pursuing impact or pursuing God?

7. What *one* thing can you commit to doing?

How Do I Decide?

Dear God, be good to me;
the sea is so wide
and my boat is so small.
—Prayer of Breton Fishermen

⁓ In previous chapters, you've read about some ways to help the needy. The sea of choices is indeed wide, and you're just one person. Unending requests from charities asking for donations and the seemingly endless opportunities to volunteer can leave you feeling very small. How do you decide which cause is the best fit for you and where to focus your energy?

DECIDE TO GIVE MONEY

One of the most practical ways to start living justice in everyday life is to fund what's really important. The possibilities for change and renewal in the world are unlimited if we all put our money where our heart is.

Christian Smith and Michael O. Emerson, authors of *Passing the Plate,* compiled a list that challenges our thinking. They tally $46 billion in lost revenue each year just from regular church attendees who don't practice biblical tithing, which is ten percent of their income. Money isn't all that's lost.

With this amount of lost revenue we could—

- Complete the funding needed to eradicate polio within the next year.
- Build 1,000,000 wells.
- Send livestock to 4,000,000 needy families.
- Give food, clothes, and shelter to *all* 6,500,000 refugees in Africa, Asia, and the Middle East.
- Triple the resources being spent on translation work to provide Bibles to the 2,737 people groups lacking Bibles in their own languages.
- Raise the salaries of the 50,000 lowest-paid pastors in the United States by $15,000 each.
- Quadruple the amount spent on global evangelism.[1]

All of these and more could be done in just one year. With unprecedented advances in worldwide technology and communication, we could do it. We could see huge gains in physical and spiritual justice in the United States and around the world. Malaria and polio could be eradicated. This is so exciting!

Only twenty-seven percent of United States Evangelicals are tithing, and thirty-six percent gave away less than two percent of their income according to a December 2008 article from *Christianity Today*.[2] What happened between the dream and the offering plate?

Decide to Worship

John Wesley wrote, "The last part of a man to be converted is his wallet."

Why is giving money so difficult?

Giving Myths

"I can't afford it."
"I'm just getting by."
"This is the best thing for my family."
"The problem is too big to fix."
"All churches and organizations misuse funds."
"I can't give because of my situation."
"The rich people give enough to carry us."

Setting the Bar Too Low

Tithing dates back as far as ancient Greece and China when spoils from war were given as religious offerings and political tribute. People gave ten percent because they could count in sets of ten easily by using their fingers.[3] We first see the biblical tithe when Abraham gives to Melchizedek, the priest. Abraham was grateful for God's provision and gave the priest ten percent of his earnings. Later the Jewish people gave tithes and offerings. Although the New Testament does not set a fixed amount of ten percent, throughout His ministry Jesus encouraged giving, and early Christians went far beyond their ability to help their own communities and other churches. The church today continues to use the tithe, not as a requirement but as a guide to help us establish guidelines for giving.

It's helpful with any religious custom to examine why we do it. Tithing provides for those who minister to us and supports their efforts to further God's kingdom locally and around the world. Unfortunately, even godly financial advisors encourage us to give without sharing why.

To be honest, the idea of tithing used to be really stressful for me. I wrote that check and felt as if I were sending money to the incinerator. I was trying to live up to the tithe standard in terms of a financial amount, but my heart-tithe was at zero.

A few years ago, when I thought of the terms "tithes" and "offerings" as interchangeable, I heard a pastor preach on giving. He explained that giving a tithe was the baseline in giving, while offerings to God went above and beyond the tithe.[4] Then he cited examples in the Bible of people giving offerings—in times of plenty to praise and thank God for His provision, as well as in times of financial hardship—out of joy for God's spiritual blessings. It changed everything for me.

I would like to say I never struggled with giving again. But that isn't true. After receiving notice that my husband would be laid off, tithing from his last remaining checks was excruciating when we didn't know when he would resume work. Aaron talked me into it after I calmed down enough to listen. That Sunday morning dur-

ing the worship service the musicians played the song "Jesus Paid
It All," by Elvina M. Hall:

> *I hear the Savior say:*
> > *"Thy strength indeed is small.*
> > *Child of weakness, watch and pray.*
> > *Find in me thine All in All."*

> *Jesus paid it all;*
> > *All to him I owe.*
> > *Sin had left a crimson stain;*
> > *He washed it white as snow.*

As we sang those words, I felt the tears come—tears of pain
and tears of joy. I paid a small amount. Jesus paid it *all*. I thought
it was about money and provision. It was about Jesus and loving
Him more, even when it's hard.

Spending Like Everyone Else

Once we get past myths and learn about biblical giving, something else seems to stop us in our tracks—the bills. House payments, car payments, insurance, education, and consumer debt
burn through paychecks to the point where we have little or no
money left for giving. How do we find a way out? It probably won't
happen overnight, and we'll need some help. Thankfully, organizations like Crown Ministries (<www.crown.org>) have a number of
great resources.

> I do not believe one can settle how much we ought to
> give. I am afraid the only safe rule is to give more than we can
> spare. In other words, if our expenditure on comforts, luxu-
> ries, amusements, etc., is up to the standard common among
> those with the same income as our own, we are probably giv-
> ing away too little. If our charities do not at all pinch or ham-
> per us, I should say they are too small (*C. S. Lewis*).

Saving as Though It's All Mine

As soon as I learn a spiritual lesson, the same vice appears
again in a different form with a different face. It's the arcade game
I loved as a child, Whac-A-Mole. Use a large soft mallet to pound

the plastic animal down before he pops up again. It was so simple. I knew what I was looking for—moles. As an adult, I now play the spiritual game "Whac-the-Greed." Easy, right? Look for overspending, and "whack" it back down into its greedy hole.

The problem is that the face of greed is not always overspending; sometimes it takes the form of over-saving. I might feel pretty good about not spending too much, but could I be going too far the other way and hoarding what I could be giving? I must ask, *God, how do you want me to use your money? I don't trust myself.* At times in my life I have been an overspender, but recently, being a more "responsible" adult, I tend to be a hoarder.

Trusting God to channel finances to the right places may be even more difficult than putting the brakes on overspending. Sound financial advice starts us out well, but we need to hand the plan over to God for ultimate approval.

DECIDE ON THE CHURCH

Once we get past our fears to make the funds available, where should the money go?

From Thieves to a Treasured Possession

The Israelites had lied, committed adultery, defrauded workers of their wages, and deprived the needy of justice. They wanted to come back to God, and this was how He wanted them to return:

"Will a man rob God? Yet you rob me.

"But you ask, 'How do we rob you?'

"In tithes and offerings. You are under a curse—the whole nation of you—because you are robbing me. Bring the whole tithe into the storehouse, that there may be food in my house. Test me in this," says the LORD Almighty, "and see if I will not throw open the floodgates of heaven and pour out so much blessing that you will not have room enough for it. I will prevent pests from devouring your crops, and the vines in your fields will not cast their fruit," says the LORD Almighty. "Then all the nations will call you blessed, for yours will be a delightful land," says the LORD Almighty.

"You have said harsh things against me," says the LORD.

"Yet you ask, 'What have we said against you?'

"You have said, 'It is futile to serve God. What did we gain by carrying out his requirements and going about like mourners before the LORD Almighty? But now we call the arrogant blessed. Certainly the evildoers prosper, and even those who challenge God escape.'"

Then those who feared the LORD talked with each other, and the LORD listened and heard. A scroll of remembrance was written in his presence concerning those who feared the LORD and honored his name.

"They will be mine," says the LORD Almighty, "in the day when I make up *my treasured possession*. I will spare them, just as in compassion a man spares his son who serves him. And you will again see the distinction between the righteous and the wicked, between those who serve God and those who do not" *(Malachi 3:8-18, emphasis added).*

Promise

When we do things God's way, He promises to show favor to us. For the Israelites, He promised to remove their curse and to bless their work. When we serve the needy, we need that blessing on our work as well.

Portrayal

God was given glory after the terrible tragedy of Hurricane Katrina on the United States Gulf coast in August 2005. Churches all across the country acted when government and bureaucracies failed. The churches helped right where they were located. Yet often the Church is known only for what it's against. Our "naughty" list of disapproval is widely shared around the world. I dream of a day when the word "Christian" brings to mind someone who promotes literacy, works to provide clean water, and cares for the broken.

In the Scripture passage you just read from Malachi, God says that we'll see the distinction between those who serve God and those who do not. Can we regain our lost distinctiveness as those who do God's work in the world?

Wouldn't it be great if when visitors came to church they saw a real difference in us? What if along with the ministries essential to running the church, such as the nursery, ushering, and Sunday School, they saw groups ministering to poor children, adopting the school down the road, visiting the sick and disabled, leading prison ministries, partnering with the local crisis pregnancy centers, helping AIDS orphans, and promoting malaria prevention?

Provision

The emphasis of the Church being the first line of defense for the needy continues into the New Testament. When first-century believers collected an offering to take care of the poor and needy, where did they take it? To the disciples. (See Acts 4:34-35.) They chose among them men who had discernment to oversee the distribution. (See Acts 6:1-4.)

The Bible gives many reasons that a person might be in need. The needs do not all look the same, nor do they have the same solutions. Poverty comes by uncontrollable circumstances and injustice, but there are other more controversial causes as well. Proverbs lists the other causes, such as laziness, lack of discipline, idleness, haste, and excess.[5]

The Bible brings level balance to the situation. But human wisdom often falls into extremes and views *all* poverty as a result of laziness or idealizes poverty as being only circumstantial or caused by injustice. Leaders with wisdom can give real help, not Band-aids or enablement. They can do this in a way that the other work of the Church is still funded and staff members are paid a fair wage. (See Acts 6; Galatians 6:6.)

Let us work together to replenish churches of the necessary resources, staff, and funding to bring justice and the gospel message to the needy.

Partnerships

The money is not just for us. Besides buildings, facilities, and staff, this money merges into a larger sum that helps the local community and global ventures as the church partners with missions, advocacy, Bible translation, and justice allies. These large support gifts build orphanages, dig wells, print Bibles, commission missionaries, and more. Church partners are screened carefully to reflect biblical values and the unique distinctives of each local church.

Prevail

I understand the temptation to give up on the Church. From the very beginning the Church, God's people, has been a flawed group. But despite the stains, we know how the story ends.

Jesus promises in Matthew 17:16-19 that nothing, not even hell, will prevail against the Church. And at the end of the story the Church is victorious, pictured as a beautiful bride, restored in Revelation 19. When all other human-made institutions have gone, the Church remains. We can be a part of something that conquers, something that lasts.

DECIDE ON YOUR PRIORITIES

Give to the Church, and keep giving to organizations doing great work in the world. Many organizations are essential partners filling in the gap with necessary funds, training, and resources. But how do we wade through all the appeals for help?

Decipher the Codes
- NPO—Nonprofit organization
- NGO—Nongovernmental organization, often used interchangeably with "NPO"
- Faith-based—an organization founded on moral principles but not necessarily associated with Christianity or another religion
- Christian-based—an organization centered on Christian values but not necessarily through evangelism
- Christian—an organization based on Christian values, and evangelism *is* incorporated into its services

"Faith-based," "Christian-based," and "Christian" are often used interchangeably to describe organizations, and are sometimes even misused by the organizations themselves. Mission statements and background facts located on organization Web sites can help clarify whether your values line up with a particular organization's mission.

Decipher the Type of Help

Something else to consider in setting your priorities is what type of help you want to support.

- Short-term relief—immediate relief in disasters, medical emergencies, and so on
- Long-term relief—programs that work to end cycles of poverty, hunger, slavery, and so on
- Sustainability support—independence for those served who eventually overcome their setback to provide for themselves and help others in their community

Sustainability is the ideal outcome to return dignity to the recipient. But some situations call for immediate relief. Hospitals have the emergency rooms as well as rehabilitation units. The same goes for relief. We need short-term workers to provide emergency care while others work to rehabilitate, which leads to self-sustainment.

Decide on a Partner

How many times have you heard, "Help out—it's for a good cause!" Have you ever wondered what that really means? Our personal preferences vary, so we won't all have the same idea about what a "good cause" is, but here are some things to think about.

Focused Giving

- Mission—what is the mission statement of an organization? What are its objectives?
- Transparency—financial integrity documenting that the money goes where it's supposed to go.

- Efficiency—a small percentage of income goes to running the organization, and most goes directly to the work at hand; the generally accepted rule is twenty percent or less to administration costs.
- Flexibility—adapts to a changing world.
- Leadership—is it the boss from the top or a group effort?
- Personal integrity—from the CEO, marketing VP, to the worker on the field—how are their personal disciplines, finances, and family relationships?
- Centrality of Christ—it can be easy to put the "good cause" at the center when the overarching principle should be "Christ in the center. This work is something we do for Him."
- Sub-causes—does this charity have connections to political parties, lobbying groups, or major corporations, such as pharmaceutical companies, media groups, and so on?
- Overall management—how organized, professional, responsive is the staff?
- Reputation—do outsiders speak well of the organization?
- Ratings—how well does the organization rate with independent sources?

Charity Watchdog Groups

It seems like a lot to take in. So wouldn't it be great if someone saved you the hours of research and pointed you to the right path?

Just as *Consumer Reports* magazine rates consumer products, charity watchdog groups help keep organizations accountable by letting you know what's going on.

Ministry Watch

Ministry Watch is the online database of Wall Watchers and gives ratings to public charities, church, and parachurch ministries.

Grading features:
- Five-star financial efficiency ratings
- Transparency grade (A, B, C, D, F)
- Analyst comments
- Financial information

Other features:
- Donor alerts (worst ratings)
- Shining Light Ministries (top-thirty list each year)
- Tips and ministry complaint forms
- Newsletters
- Articles
  <www.ministrywatch.org>
  <www.wallwatchers.org>

Charity Navigator

Charity navigator is a database that evaluates more than 5,000 of the most popular American nonprofits.

Grading features:
- Overall four-star rating
- Efficiency four-star rating
- Capacity (Can it sustain its efforts over time?) four-star rating
- Historical data
- Public comments
- News about the charity

Other features:
- Top-ten lists
- Monthly e-newsletter
- Tips and resources
- Blog
  <www.charitynavigators.org>

Evangelical Council for Financial Accountability (ECFA)

Membership accreditation is often conveyed by the ECFA seal on organization Web sites and materials. In the Christian world this is similar to the reputable Better Business Bureau standing. Members must pay a fee and then submit to a field review and board standards by the ECFA. Smaller organizations that can't join due to membership fees and costly certified public accountant audits may join as affiliate members.

Mercy Rising Charitable Organization Appendix

Does it still seem like a lot of work to you? If you turn to the Charitable Organization Appendix in the back of this book, you'll see a table that lists a few reputable organizations by sector and ministry type. It also then lists their Ministry Watch, Charity Navigator, and ECFA standings at the time this book was completed. Hopefully this will be helpful to you and save you hours of research.

Disclaimer

Please note that this is not meant to be a competitive ranking grid, and there may be many other worthwhile charities beyond those listed. For updated information, please check the charity watchdogs' Web sites.

DECIDE TO INVEST

Investing the time to take a close look at a charity before you give may seem quite time-consuming, but it's part of being financially responsible, just as are budgeting, buying insurance, or saving for the future. It's more than just giving—it's an investment. When I *give,* I feel as if I'm sending money to outer space, never to be seen again. When I *invest,* I carefully choose a plan and watch expectantly for a return.

Do you need more help?

- *The Eternity Portfolio,* by Alan Gotthardt
- *Raising Money-Smart Kids,* by Ron and Judy Blue
- *The Treasure Principle,* by Randy Alcorn
- Royal Treasure: a money web site for women. Collect information, strategize, and connect with other women about financial issues based on biblical principles.
  <www.royaltreasure.org>
- Generous Giving: This Web site challenges readers to give extravagantly. It includes practical resources and stories of real people moving past their fears to experiencing joyful giving.
  <www.generousgiving.org>

- The National Christian Foundation: This organization fur-
  thers Christian stewardship by setting up funds, trusts,
  scholarships, annuities, endowments, and more.
  <www.nationalchristian.com>

Invest in People

No matter what strategies we employ or how careful we become, we must make sure we rely on God's leading in our lives.
Investing not only leads us to the right partners—it leads us back
to individual care for people.

Charles Dickens' brilliant writing brought the characters alive
in *A Christmas Carol*. As a child, I was captivated by the love interest of young Ebenezer Scrooge. As an adult, however, Mr. Fezziwig wins my heart. *Who?* He's the character who employed young
Scrooge and financed the famous Christmas party. He treated his
wife and workers with respect and generosity. He used his money,
time, and kind words to invest in people.

I have started to notice the "Fezziwigs" around me—those who
have invested their time and finances in my life. I try to remember
to thank them and, in turn, be a "Fezziwig" to someone else. To
celebrate and share not just during calendar holidays with my immediate family but also in my treatment of others who are in need.

Because I've been a recipient of God's extravagant grace, how
can I not join in the celebration?

Command those who are rich in this present world not to
be arrogant nor to put their hope in wealth, which is so uncertain, but to put their hope in God, who richly provides us with
everything for our enjoyment. Command them to do good, to
be rich in good deeds, and to be generous and willing to share.
In this way they will lay up treasure for themselves as a firm
foundation for the coming age, so they may take hold of the
life which is truly life. *(1 Timothy 6:17-19).*

Not because I have to, but because I get to.

Not in fear, but in fun.

Not getting by, but really living.

Decide to Act

In the Book of Malachi, when the Israelites turned back to God, they wrote down their commitment. Like them, we easily forget. Take some time to look back over previous chapters and your reflection answers. Then fill in the ONE Action Plan below. Don't put it off. Put your plan into action today.

One Action Plan
Reflection Questions Summary

Find the "*one* thing question" from each chapter, and record your answers in the spaces below.

Part I. Getting Real About Giving

1. Why Justice? Why Me? _____
2. Love Thing _____
3. Daily Bread _____

Part II. The *One* Thing I Can Do

4. At Home _____
5. Shopping _____
6. It's Just Business _____
7. Space Invaders _____
8. Away from Home _____

Part III. Reality Check

9. Real Mess, Real Rewards _____
10. How Do I Decide? _____

ACTION STEPS

Use the answers above to continue narrowing your focus.

Part I. Getting Real About Giving

What is the *one* thing I can change about my thinking or my emotions toward the needy or giving? _____

Part II. The One Thing I Can Do

What is the *one* thing I will do? _____

Who of my friends, family, or other groups I'm a part of can I take with me? List specific people. _____

Part III. Reality Check

What is my *one* goal to be more effective financially in Kingdom work? _____

What is my *one* partner organization or church? _____

One Thing

Which action step from the previous list can I start first? _____

Commit to Persevere

Service is rewarding as well as difficult. I will ask _____[name] to pray for me and hold me accountable to my commitment to begin my one thing by _____[date]_____.

MERCY RISING

See! The winter is past; the rains are over and gone.
Flowers appear on the earth; the season of singing has come.
—Song of Songs 2:11-12

Every spring my husband and I look forward to our weekend away. It's the end of a long school year. I've poured myself into scales, chords, and classical pieces for my students, culminating with the end-of-the-year recital. I've rejoiced with them in their successes and struggled with them in difficult repertoire. I don't want to hear another Für Elise—at least, not for a few months. Aaron has finished a spring musical production at church with long hours, extra rehearsals, and a weekend of nonstop performances. This weekend the stress is behind us.

After the dark winter, I miss my old friend *sunrise*. By now the dawn peers through the slanted cracks in the curtains. Emotionally spent, I sit on the deck overlooking the pastel tree line of the state park. Gorgeous fields and wispy wildflowers rise and fall with the spring winds along the forest's edge.

Beyond those waving trees I hear the forests, cries of the hawk and robin, sounds of insects and distant automobiles—sounds I could have heard at home, but I didn't listen. If we could hear into the human hearts beyond the tree lines fanning out from the porch to the United States and to the world, what would we hear?

Beyond my voice and the voices of the other women you've heard, what would the voices of those who need justice say? Some voices cry in despair. Some are silenced by fatigue. But still others sing, ringing with dignity and hope.

Song of Despair

Shout it aloud, do not hold back. Raise your voice like a trumpet. Declare to my people their rebellion and to the house of Jacob their sins.

For day after day they seek me out; they seem eager to know my ways, as if they were a nation that does what is right and has not forsaken the commands of its God. They ask me for just decisions and seem eager for God to come near them.

"Why have we fasted," they say, "and you have not seen it? Why have we humbled ourselves and you have not noticed?"

Yet on the day of your fasting, you do as you please and exploit all your workers. Your fasting ends in quarreling and strife, and in striking each other with wicked fists. You cannot fast as you do today and expect your voice to be heard on high (*Isaiah 58:1-4*).

I feel so sick and tired after a day's work that I do not want to work the next day. But hunger does not allow thinking of sickness. The thought of living with an empty stomach makes everything else forgotten. We work to save ourselves from hunger (woman in a Bangladesh sweatshop).[1]

We are left tied [up] like straw (a discussion group, Dibdibe Wajtu, Ethiopia).[2]

Is this the kind of fast I have chosen, only a day for a man to humble himself? Is it only for bowing one's head like a reed and for lying on sackcloth and ashes? Is that what you call a fast, a day acceptable to the LORD? (*Isaiah 58:5*).

I repeat that we need water as badly as we need air (woman, Tash-Bulak, Kyrgyz Republic).[3]

My husband is not working and has taken to heavy drinking, especially akpeteshie [a strong alcoholic drink brewed locally]. I have to feed and clothe him, in addition to my children. All this makes life very hard since my income is not much anymore. At times I find it very difficult to pay for my children's school fees.

My hope and future are in their education . . . for the time when I am old and can't work any longer. My children have seen how I've suffered to educate them so they won't end up like their father and me. I am doing my best so that in the future they will let me enjoy the benefits of my hard work (Ghanaian woman).[4]

Hope

Is not this the kind of fasting I have chosen: to loose the chains of injustice and untie the cords of the yoke, to set the oppressed free and break every yoke? (*Isaiah 58:6*).

Today my family and I are free, and I am glad to share with you my story. I am not a slave anymore.

I can eat in peace, and my grandchildren are going to school. I can spend time with them like you do. I have the joy of watching them grow up in freedom. I tell them to study hard.

I can dream of a good life in freedom, and I am living one. Initially I was afraid of this transition to freedom, because we didn't know any other work, and I was afraid the owner would beat us.

But today I am very happy, and I live in peace. We are respected members of the community. We have cattle now, and we are earning money from them. We do not have a lot of possessions, but it is enough because we are free (freed female slave in south Asia).[5]

Is it not to share your food with the hungry and to provide the poor wanderer with shelter—when you see the naked, to clothe him, and not to turn away from your own flesh and blood? (*Isaiah 58:7*).

Something will happen; otherwise, why have you come? (slum dweller, Bangladesh, 1995)[6]

Healing Light

Then your light will break forth like the dawn, and your healing will quickly appear; Then your righteousness will go before you, and the glory of the Lord will be your rear guard (Isaiah 58:8).

We were escorted one and a half hours by police/military escort to a small village. . . . When the door to the van opened, there were over two hundred people waiting for us. There were at least fifty in wheelchairs that had been assembled the night before and early this day. I will always remember the astonished looks on the faces of those sitting in these newly assembled chairs. Some had smiles that were from ear to ear. There was one gentleman who had placed both his homemade artificial legs on the ground beside his chair. That is one of the great visions I will always keep with me (workers in east Asia).[7]

I was walking in a deadly area, but someone read the sign that said, "There are mines here!" I could be dead if it weren't for that person. Now, if I knew how to read, that situation could be avoided. Now, I am not going to commit myself to death—because I *can* read (literate Angolan woman).[8]

You will call and the LORD will answer; you will cry for help, and he will say: Here am I (Isaiah 58:9).

The PSB went to my prison interrogating, threatening, and harassing me numerous times. They even directed other prisoners to take off all my clothes and forced me to stand alone outside in the evening without letting me sleep. . . . During these terrible circumstances, I prayed without ceasing. I asked God to give me strength. Every time when my son came to visit me and shared with me that brothers and sisters from all over the world had been praying for me, I felt greatly strengthened and empowered, which has enabled me to continue to live (freed religious prisoner from China).[9]

Do away with the yoke of oppression, with the pointing finger and malicious talk (*Isaiah 58:9*).

I praise the Lord because He had mercy on me. I now have a place I call home. I now know God better than before. I have hope.

The Lord rescued me from the pit of darkness and brought me to light. I wished to die, but God was with my life. I prayed God to hold my life safe, and he did it. God gave me a good mum who meets my needs. He gave me a place where I can sleep, and something I can feed on. God has a good plan for me in my future (a destitute boy who now has food, shelter, clothing, and education).[10]

If you spend yourselves in behalf of the hungry and satisfy the needs of the oppressed, then your light will rise in the darkness, and your night will become like the noonday.

The LORD will guide you always; he will satisfy your needs in a sun-scorched land and will strengthen your frame (*Isaiah 58:10-11*).

I greet you in the name of Jesus Christ and hope you are doing well. I would like to inform you that my mother received Jesus as her personal Savior. . . . Pray with me that I may perform well in my studies. . . . God bless you very much (letter excerpt from our sponsored child in Tanzania).

You will be like a well-watered garden, like a spring whose waters never fail (*Isaiah 58:11*).

The children made a mad dash for the water, drinking, bathing, and basking in their refreshment. Like liquid magic, joy swept the crowd.

The water gushing out was naturally filtered and free from parasites. Together we drank, and though I had known it would be clean water, I'm not sure I ever imagined it would be this clean. Every last one of us should have access to this kind of clean water (reports from Rwanda).[11]

The Heights/Rebuilding

Your people will rebuild the ancient ruins and will raise up the age-old foundations; you will be called Repairer of Broken Walls, Restorer of Streets with Dwellings (*Isaiah 58:12*).

If somebody could encourage me, and at the end of the encouragement I have achieved a home, then why can't I do it to somebody else? This is what life is all about. This is what Christianity is all about. We all have to help somebody (woman from Guyana who continues to volunteer building homes for others)[12]

"Then you will find your joy in the LORD, and I will cause you to ride on the heights of the land and to feast on the inheritance of your father Jacob." The mouth of the LORD has spoken (*Isaiah 58:14*).

Only the redemptive love could turn a canyon of despair into a mountaintop of triumph. Only Christ could use the broken and sick to be mercy for the wounds of the world. Only He could resurrect us from the winter of our apathy to the spring of our hope. Only mercy could transform cries in the darkness to songs of life.

After we had lunch with them, they sang for us. It's really amazing how they used songs to express themselves and their thoughts, expectations, fears, and anxieties. The words of the final song were—

Here they are, yes we agree, here they are, our visitors . . . yes, here they are, they are here to help us and we hope they won't forget us.

Will we remember?[13] (World Bank researchers in South Africa 1998).

The time for inaction is past.

The time for despair is over.

The time for apathy is done.

Look at the good work being done.

Feel the story of renewal.

Listen—the time for singing has come.

Appendix A

Justice Scriptures

Here are about 100 of the over 2,500 Bible verses relating to justice!

Exodus 22:22   Do not take advantage of a widow or an orphan.

Exodus 23:6   Do not deny justice to your poor people in their lawsuits.

Exodus 23:11   . . . but during the seventh year let the land lie unplowed and unused. Then the poor among your people may get food from it, and the wild animals may eat what they leave. Do the same with your vineyard and your olive grove.

Leviticus 19:10   Do not go over your vineyard a second time or pick up the grapes that have fallen. Leave them for the poor and the alien. I am the Lord your God.

Leviticus 19:15   Do not pervert justice; do not show partiality to the poor or favoritism to the great, but judge your neighbor fairly.

Leviticus 23:22   When you reap the harvest of your land, do not reap to the very edges of your field or gather the gleanings of your harvest. Leave them for the poor and the alien. I am the Lord your God.

Leviticus 25:25   If one of your countrymen becomes poor and sells some of his property, his nearest relative is to come and redeem what his countryman has sold.

Leviticus 25:35   If one of your countrymen becomes poor and is unable to support himself among you, help him as you would an alien or a temporary resident, so he can continue to live among you.

Leviticus 25:39   If one of your countrymen becomes poor among you and sells himself to you, do not make him work as a slave.

Leviticus 25:47-48   If an alien or a temporary resident among you becomes rich and one of your countrymen becomes poor and sells himself to the alien living among you or to a member of the alien's clan, he retains the right of redemption...

Deuteronomy 10:18   He defends the cause of the fatherless and the widow, and loves the alien, giving him food and clothing.

Deuteronomy 14:28-29   At the end of every three years, bring all the tithes of that year's produce and store it in your towns, so that the Levites (who have no allotment or inheritance of their own) and the aliens, the fatherless and the widows who live in your towns may come and eat and be satisfied, and so that the Lord your God may bless you in all the work of your hands.

Deuteronomy 15:4   However, there should be no poor among you, for in the land the Lord your God is giving you to possess as your inheritance, he will richly bless you . . .

Deuteronomy 15:7   If there is a poor man among your brothers in any of the towns of the land that the Lord your God is giving you, do not be hardhearted or tightfisted toward your poor brother.

Deuteronomy 15:9   Be careful not to harbor this wicked thought: "The seventh year, the year for canceling debts, is near," so that you do not show ill will toward your needy brother and give him nothing. He may then appeal to the Lord against you, and you will be found guilty of sin.

Deuteronomy 15:10	Give generously to him and do so without a grudging heart; then because of this the LORD your God will bless you in all your work and in everything you put your hand to.
Deuteronomy 15:11	There will always be poor people in the land. Therefore I command you to be openhanded toward your brothers and toward the poor and needy in your land.
Deuteronomy 24:14	Do not take advantage of a hired man who is poor and needy, whether he is a brother Israelite or an alien living in one of your towns.
Deuteronomy 24:17	Do not deprive the alien or the fatherless of justice, or take the cloak of the widow as a pledge.
Deuteronomy 24:19-21	When you are harvesting in your field and you overlook a sheaf, do not go back to get it. Leave it for the alien, the fatherless and the widow, so that the LORD your God may bless you in all the work of your hands. When you beat the olives from your trees, do not go over the branches a second time. Leave what remains for the alien, the fatherless and the widow. When you harvest the grapes in your vineyard, do not go over the vines again. Leave what remains for the alien, the fatherless and the widow.
Deuteronomy 27:19	"Cursed is the man who withholds justice from the alien, the fatherless or the widow." Then all the people shall say, "Amen!"
1 Samuel 2:8	He raises the poor from the dust and lifts the needy from the ash heap; he seats them with princes and has them inherit a throne of honor.
Esther 9:22	. . . as the time when the Jews got relief from their enemies, and as the month when their sorrow was turned into joy and their mourning into a day of celebration. He wrote them to observe the days as days of feasting and joy and giving presents of food to one another and gifts to the poor.
Job 24:14	When daylight is gone, the murderer rises up and kills the poor and needy; in the night he steals forth like a thief.
Job 29:12	. . . because I rescued the poor who cried for help, and the fatherless who had none to assist him.
Job 30:25	Have I not wept for those in trouble? Has not my soul grieved for the poor?
Job 31:16	If I have denied the desires of the poor or let the eyes of the widow grow weary,
Psalm 9:9	The LORD is a refuge for the oppressed, a stronghold in times of trouble.
Psalm 9:18	But the needy will not always be forgotten, nor the hope of the afflicted ever perish.
Psalm 12:5	"Because of the oppression of the weak and the groaning of the needy, I will now arise," says the LORD. "I will protect them from those who malign them."
Psalm 14:6	You evildoers frustrate the plans of the poor, but the LORD is their refuge.
Psalm 34:6	This poor man called, and the LORD heard him; he saved him out of all his troubles.
Psalm 35:10	My whole being will exclaim, "Who is like you, O LORD ? You rescue the poor from those too strong for them, the poor and needy from those who rob them."
Psalm 37:14	The wicked draw the sword and bend the bow to bring down the poor and needy, to slay those whose ways are upright.
Psalm 40:17	Yet I am poor and needy; may the LORD think of me. You are my help and my deliverer; O my God, do not delay.

Psalm 68:5	A father to the fatherless, a defender of widows, is God in his holy dwelling.
Psalm 68:10	Your people settled in it, and from your bounty, O God, you provided for the poor.
Psalm 69:32-33	The poor will see and be glad—you who seek God, may your hearts live! The LORD hears the needy and does not despise his captive people.
Psalm 70:5	Yet I am poor and needy; come quickly to me, O God. You are my help and my deliverer; O LORD, do not delay.
Psalm 72:4	He will defend the afflicted among the people and save the children of the needy; he will crush the oppressor.
Psalm 72:12-13	For he will deliver the needy who cry out, the afflicted who have no one to help. He will take pity on the weak and the needy and save the needy from death.
Psalm 74:21	Do not let the oppressed retreat in disgrace; may the poor and needy praise your name.
Psalm 82:3-4	Defend the cause of the weak and fatherless; maintain the rights of the poor and oppressed. Rescue the weak and needy; deliver them from the hand of the wicked.
Psalm 107:41	But he lifted the needy out of their affliction and increased their families like flocks.
Psalm 109:31	For he stands at the right hand of the needy one, to save his life from those who condemn him.
Psalm 112:9	He has scattered abroad his gifts to the poor, his righteousness endures forever; his horn will be lifted high in honor.
Psalm 113:7	He raises the poor from the dust and lifts the needy from the ash heap.
Psalm 132:15	I will bless her with abundant provisions; her poor will I satisfy with food.
Psalm 140:12	I know that the LORD secures justice for the poor and upholds the cause of the needy.
Psalm 146:7	He upholds the cause of the oppressed and gives food to the hungry. The LORD sets prisoners free . . .
Psalm 146:9	The LORD watches over the alien and sustains the fatherless and the widow, but he frustrates the ways of the wicked.
Proverbs 13:23	A poor man's field may produce abundant food, but injustice sweeps it away.
Proverbs 14:21	He who despises his neighbor sins, but blessed is he who is kind to the needy.
Proverbs 14:31	He who oppresses the poor shows contempt for their Maker, but whoever is kind to the needy honors God.
Proverbs 15:25	The LORD tears down the proud man's house but he keeps the widow's boundaries intact.
Proverbs 16:19	Better to be lowly in spirit and among the oppressed than to share plunder with the proud.
Proverbs 17:5	He who mocks the poor shows contempt for their Maker; whoever gloats over disaster will not go unpunished.

Proverbs 19:17	He who is kind to the poor lends to the Lord, and he will reward him for what he has done.
Proverbs 21:13	If a man shuts his ears to the cry of the poor, he too will cry out and not be answered.
Proverbs 22:9	A generous man will himself be blessed, for he shares his food with the poor.
Proverbs 22:16	He who oppresses the poor to increase his wealth and he who gives gifts to the rich—both come to poverty.
Proverbs 22:22	Do not exploit the poor because they are poor and do not crush the needy in court…
Proverbs 28:3	A ruler who oppresses the poor is like a driving rain that leaves no crops.
Proverbs 28:27	He who gives to the poor will lack nothing, but he who closes his eyes to them receives many curses.
Proverbs 29:7	The righteous care about justice for the poor, but the wicked have no such concern.
Proverbs 30:14	. . . those whose teeth are swords and whose jaws are set with knives to devour the poor from the earth, the needy from among mankind.
Proverbs 31:9	Speak up and judge fairly; defend the rights of the poor and needy.
Proverbs 31:20	She opens her arms to the poor and extends her hands to the needy.
Ecclesiastes 5:8	If you see the poor oppressed in a district, and justice and rights denied, do not be surprised at such things; for one official is eyed by a higher one, and over them both are others higher still.
Isaiah 1:17	. . . learn to do right! Seek justice, encourage the oppressed. Defend the cause of the fatherless, plead the case of the widow.
Isaiah 3:14-15	The Lord enters into judgment against the elders and leaders of his people: "It is you who have ruined my vineyard; the plunder from the poor is in your houses. What do you mean by crushing my people and grinding the faces of the poor?" declares the Lord, the Lord Almighty.
Isaiah 10:2	. . . to deprive the poor of their rights and withhold justice from the oppressed of my people, making widows their prey and robbing the fatherless.
Isaiah 11:4	but with righteousness he will judge the needy, with justice he will give decisions for the poor of the earth. He will strike the earth with the rod of his mouth; with the breath of his lips he will slay the wicked.
Isaiah 14:30	The poorest of the poor will find pasture, and the needy will lie down in safety. But your root I will destroy by famine; it will slay your survivors.
Ezekiel 22:29	The people of the land practice extortion and commit robbery; they oppress the poor and needy and mistreat the alien, denying them justice.
Amos 2:6-7	This is what the Lord says: "For three sins of Israel, even for four, I will not turn back {my wrath}. They sell the righteous for silver, and the needy for a pair of sandals. They trample on the heads of the poor as upon the dust of the ground and deny justice to the oppressed. Father and son use the same girl and so profane my holy name.
Amos 4:1	Hear this word, you cows of Bashan on Mount Samaria, you women who oppress the poor and crush the needy and say to your husbands, "Bring us some drinks!"

Amos 8:4	Hear this, you who trample the needy and do away with the poor of the land,
Amos 8:6	. . . buying the poor with silver and the needy for a pair of sandals, selling even the sweepings with the wheat.
Zechariah 7:10	Do not oppress the widow or the fatherless, the alien or the poor. In your hearts do not think evil of each other.
Malachi 3:5	"So I will come near to you for judgment. I will be quick to testify against sorcerers, adulterers and perjurers, against those who defraud laborers of their wages, who oppress the widows and the fatherless, and deprive aliens of justice, but do not fear me," says the Lord Almighty.
Matthew 19:21	Jesus answered, "If you want to be perfect, go, sell your possessions and give to the poor, and you will have treasure in heaven. Then come, follow me."
Matthew 25:35	"For I was hungry and you gave me something to eat, I was thirsty and you gave me something to drink, I was a stranger and you invited me in."
Mark 12:40	"They devour widows' houses and for a show make lengthy prayers. Such men will be punished most severely."
Luke 4:18	"The Spirit of the Lord is on me, because he has anointed me to preach good news to the poor. He has sent me to proclaim freedom for the prisoners and recovery of sight for the blind, to release the oppressed."
Luke 7:22	So he replied to the messengers, "Go back and report to John what you have seen and heard: The blind receive sight, the lame walk, those who have leprosy are cured, the deaf hear, the dead are raised, and the good news is preached to the poor."
Luke 12:33	"Sell your possessions and give to the poor. Provide purses for yourselves that will not wear out, a treasure in heaven that will not be exhausted, where no thief comes near and no moth destroys."
Luke 14:13	"But when you give a banquet, invite the poor, the crippled, the lame, the blind."
Luke 18:22	When Jesus heard this, he said to him, "You still lack one thing. Sell everything you have and give to the poor, and you will have treasure in heaven. Then come, follow me."
John 12:5-6	"Why wasn't this perfume sold and the money given to the poor? It was worth a year's wages." He did not say this because he cared about the poor but because he was a thief; as keeper of the money bag, he used to help himself to what was put into it.
Acts 9:36	In Joppa there was a disciple named Tabitha (which, when translated, is Dorcas), who was always doing good and helping the poor.
Acts 10:4	Cornelius stared at him in fear. "What is it, Lord?" he asked. The angel answered, "Your prayers and gifts to the poor have come up as a memorial offering before God."
Acts 24:17	"After an absence of several years, I came to Jerusalem to bring my people gifts for the poor and to present offerings."
Romans 12:20	On the contrary: "If your enemy is hungry, feed him; if he is thirsty, give him something to drink. In doing this, you will heap burning coals on his head."
Romans 15:26	For Macedonia and Achaia were pleased to make a contribution for the poor among the saints in Jerusalem.

Galatians 2:10	All they asked was that we should continue to remember the poor, the very thing I was eager to do.
1 Timothy 5:3	Give proper recognition to those widows who are really in need.
James 1:27	Religion that God our Father accepts as pure and faultless is this: to look after orphans and widows in their distress and to keep oneself from being polluted by the world.
James 2:2-6	Suppose a man comes into your meeting wearing a gold ring and fine clothes, and a poor man in shabby clothes also comes in. If you show special attention to the man wearing fine clothes and say, "Here's a good seat for you," but say to the poor man, "You stand there" or "Sit on the floor by my feet," have you not discriminated among yourselves and become judges with evil thoughts? Listen, my dear brothers: Has not God chosen those who are poor in the eyes of the world to be rich in faith and to inherit the kingdom he promised those who love him? But you have insulted the poor. Is it not the rich who are exploiting you? Are they not the ones who are dragging you into court?
1 John 3:17-18	If anyone has material possessions and sees his brother in need but has no pity on him, how can the love of God be in him? Dear children, let us not love with words or tongue but with actions and in truth.

Appendix B

Stop Human Trafficking

To report abuse call the National Human Trafficking Resource Center, at 1-888-3737-888, or 911 in an emergency.

What is trafficking?

Holding someone by physical force or threats.
Using the person for work or sex.
It is illegal.
It happens in our communities and around the world, victimizing non-USA nationals at a higher rate.

How to spot human trafficking

Beauty or massage parlor employees

They seem reluctant, frightened, or in pain.
They are able to keep little or none of the money they receive from clients.
They have little or no time off.
They are not allowed breaks.

Restaurant, farming, or factory workers

Workers are given poor safety equipment, work clothes, and accommodations.
They have no identification or mailing address.
They have no days off or vacation time.
They are picked up and dropped off in vans at unusual hours of the day.
They seem afraid.

Domestic laborers

They are rarely allowed out of the house unless their employers or guardians are with them.
They do not have proper accommodations, food, or breaks.

They are not treated well by the family: ignored, abused, threatened.
A child you may see who is traveling

The child is traveling alone.
The child has few belongings but does have a cell phone.
The child behaves unusually or inappropriately—fearful, lost, or sexual.

People in your city
Young, elderly, or disabled foreign nationals who are begging in public places or on public transport.
They show signs of verbal or physical abuse.
A large group of children with only one adult as guardian.

You or someone you know
A teenage girl in a relationship with an older man who buys her gifts or illegal substances.
She shows signs of being controlled by verbal, physical, or sexual abuse.
She is taken from her family home and returned after varying lengths of time. Her relationship with her family or guardians becomes severed.

Source: "Stop the Traffik USA," *STOP THE TRAFFIK,*
<www.stopthetraffik.org/getinvolved/resources> (accessed April 2009).

APPENDIX C

CHARITABLE ORGANIZATION RESOURCE GUIDE

Relief and Development

Name	Ministry Area	Ministry Watch			Charity Navigator		ECFA	Web site Address
		FE	TG	SL	Overall	ER		
Floresta USA, Inc.	agriculture	4	A	•	4	4	•	www.floresta.org
Childcare Worldwide/ Childcare International	children	5	A		4	4	•	www.childcareworldwide.org
Children's Hunger Fund/CHF	children	5	A	•	4	4	•	www.chfus.org
Children's Medical Ministries	children	4	A	•	-	-		www.childmed.org
Compassion International, Inc.	children	3	A	•	4	4	•	www.compassion.com
Music for Life Institute	children	4	A		3	4		www.africanchildrenschoir.com
World Vision, Inc., US	children	4	A		3	4	•	www.worldvision.org
Christian Aid Ministries	disaster	4	A		2	4	•	www.anabaptists.org/places/cam
Christian Blind Mission/CBM	healthcare	5	A		4	4	•	www.cbmus.org
Free Wheelchair Mission	healthcare	3	A	•	4	4	•	www.freewheelchairmission.org
International Aid, Inc./IA	healthcare	5	A	•	4	4	•	www.internationalaid.org
MAP International	healthcare	5	A		4	4	•	www.map.org
Medical Teams International (MTI)	healthcare	5	A	•	3	4	•	www.medicalteams.org
Mercy Ships	healthcare	3	A	•	2	3	•	www.mercyships.org
The Luke Society, Inc.	healthcare	4	A		-	-	•	www.lukesociety.org
AMOR Ministries, Inc.	housing	3	A		-	-	•	www.amor.org
Shelter for Life, International	housing	4	B		-	-	•	www.shelter.org
Alfalit International, Inc.	literacy	5	B		-	-		www.alfalit.org
Enterprise Development International	microenterprise	2	A	•	1	2	•	www.endpoverty.org
Opportunity International	microenterprise	3	A		4	3		www.opportunity.org
Buckner Orphan Care	orphans	-	-		-	-		www.buckner.org
Christian Alliance for Orphans	orphans	-	-		-	-		www.christianalliancefororphans.org
Cry of the Orphan	orphans	-	-		-	-		www.cryoftheorphan.org
Shaohannah's Hope	orphans	-	-		-	-	•	www.showhope.org
Warm Blankets Orphan Care International	orphans	-	-		4	4	•	www.warmblankets.org
Bright Hope International	poverty	3	A		4	4	•	www.brighthope.org
Christian Appalachian Project	poverty	5	A		4	4		www.christianapp.org
Christian Relief Fund	poverty	4	A		2	4	•	www.christianrelieffund.org
Food for the Hungry, Inc.	poverty	4	A	•	3	4	•	www.fh.org
Mercy Corps	poverty	4	A		4	4		www.mercycorps.org
Samaritan's Purse/Operation Christmas Child	relief	4	A		4	4	•	www.samaritanspurse.org
World Emergency Relief/ Children's Food Fund	relief	5	A		3	4	•	www.worldemergencyrelief.org
World Help	relief	5	A	•	4	4	•	www.worldhelp.net
World Relief	relief	4	A		3	4	•	www.wr.org
Living Water International	water	3	A	•	4	3	•	www.water.cc
Water for Life, Inc.	water	2	A		-	-	•	www.wflhaiti.com
Water Missions International	water	3	A		4	4	•	www.watermissions.org
Military Community Youth Ministries (MCYM)	youth	5	A	•	4	4		www.mcym.org

Youth With A Mission (YWAM)	youth	-	-		1	4	•	www.ywam.org

Foreign Missions

Name	Ministry Area	Ministry Watch			Charity Navigator		ECFA	Web site Address
		FE	TG	SL	Overall	ER		
JAARS, Inc.	Bible translation	3	A	•	-	-	•	www.jaars.org
Wycliffe Bible Translators/WBT	Bible translation	3	A	•	-	-	•	www.wycliffe.org
Trans World Radio (TWR)	radio	3	A	•	-	-	•	www.twr.org
Fellowship International Mission	sending	4	A	•	-	-	•	www.fim.org
Turkish World Outreach (TWO)	Turkic people	4	A	•	-	-	•	www.two-fot.org
New Directions International/NDI	unreached	NR	A	•	3	4	•	www.newdirections.org
New Tribes Mission (NTM)	unreached	4	A	•	-	-		www.ntm.org

Advocacy

Name	Ministry Area	Ministry Watch			Charity Navigator		ECFA	Web site Address
		FE	TG	SL	Overall	ER		
American Family Association, Inc.	family	3	A		4	4	•	www.afa.net
Family Research Council, Inc.	family	3	A	•	3	4	•	www.frc.org
The Rutherford Institute	human rights	2	A		2	4		www.rutherford.org
Advocates International	legal	5	A		2	3	•	www.advocatesinternational.org
Alliance Defense Fund, Inc.	religious freedom	2	A		4	3	•	www.alliancedefensefund.org
American Center for Law and Justice (ACLJ)	religious freedom	5	A		-	-		www.aclj.org
Christian Legal Society/CLS	religious freedom	4	A	•	3	3	•	www.clsnet.org
Christian Freedom International (CFI)	persecution	2	A		2	2	•	www.christianfreedom.org
International Christian Concern	persecution	-	-		4	4	•	www.persecution.org
Open Doors USA	persecution	-	-		4	4	•	www.opendoorsusa.org
Persecution Project Foundation	persecution	4	A		3	4	•	www.persecutionproject.org
The Voice of the Martyrs/VOM	persecution	4	A	•	4	4	•	www.vom.org
Breakthrough, Inc.	prayer	NR	A		-	-	•	www.intercessors.org
Intercessors for America, Inc.	prayer	3	A		2	3	•	www.ifapray.org
Care Net	pregnancy	2	A	•	2	1	•	www.care-net.org
Life Centers	pregnancy	2	A	•	-	-		www.lifecenters.com
Evangelicals for Social Action, Inc.	public policy	-	-		-	-	•	www.esa-online.org
Bridges for Peace, Inc./BFPUSA	racial	3	A	•	3	4	•	www.bfpusa.org
International Fellowship of Christians and Jews	racial	3	A		3	2		www.ifcj.org
International Justice Mission/IJM	trafficking	2	A		3	3	•	www.ijm.org

Prison

Name	Ministry Area	Ministry Watch			Charity Navigator		ECFA	Web site Address
		FE	TG	SL	Overall	ER		
Good News Jail and Prison Ministry	prison	4	A	•	-	-	•	www.goodnewsjail.org
Prison Fellowship Ministries/PFM	prison	2	A	•	2	3	•	www.pfm.org

Key:

Ministry Watch
FE = Financial Efficiency (out of 5 stars)
TG = Transparency Grade (A through F)
SL = Shining Light (one of MW's top 30)
- = Organization not listed
NR = Organization listed but not rated

Charity Navigator
Overall (out of 4 stars)
ER = Efficiency Rating (out of 4 stars)
- = Organization not listed
NR = Organization listed but not rated

ECFA (Evangelical Council for Financial Accountability)
• = Member

Appendix D

Letter-Writing Guidelines

Who

    Media (letters to the editor, websites, social networking)
    Government officials
    Corporations
    Organizations

Why

    To influence change

How

    Be clear and brief.
    Establish your role: parent, consumer, business owner, or board member.
    Write how this issue or policy affects you personally.
    Explain why this issue should concern the recipient.
    Define a specific action step or outcome you would like.
    Write by hand—handwritten notes get more attention than form letters or e-mails.
    Be courteous.
    Verify the correct mailing address of the recipient, and sign your name and address.

Source: <http://relocalize.net/letter_writing_guidelines> (accessed May 2009)

Notes

Chapter 1

1. Ronald J. Sider, *Just Generosity* (Grand Rapids: Baker Books, 2007), 34-35.

2. Compassion International, Poverty Wheel, <www.compassion.com/poverty-wheel>, accessed Nnov., 2007.

3. Tony Hall, "Perspectives: Global Food Aid," *Religion and Ethics Newsweekly,* May 30, 2008, episode no. 1139, <http://www.pbs.org/wnet/religionandethics/episodes/episode-no-1139/perspectives-global-food-aid/58>, accessed August 2008.

4. *Webster's New Millennium Dictionary of English, Preview Edition,* s.v. "social justice." <http://dictionary.reference.com/browse/social justice>, accessed April 2009.

Chapter 2

1. Chad Amour Film, *The Shadows of Virtue,* Humdinger Pictures, 2007.

2. C. S. Lewis, *The Problem of Pain* (Nashville: B & H Publishing Group, 1999).

3. Mark Helprin, *Winter's Tale* (Orlando, Fla.: Harcourt Brace Jovanovich, 1983), 169.

4. Ken Gire, *Intense Moments with the Savior, Learning to Feel* (Grand Rapids: Zondervan Publishing House, 1994), xii.

5. Robert Lupton, *Compassion, Justice and the Christian Life: Rethinking Ministry to the Poor* (Ventura, Calif.: Regal Books, 2007).

Chapter 3

1. Dale Hanson Bourke, *The Skeptic's Guide to Global Poverty* (Colorado Springs: Authentic Books, 2007), 65.

2. "Gratitude," in Nichole Nordeman, *Woven and Spun* songbook (Milwaukee: Hal Leonard, Ariose and Mark Hammond Music, 2002), 74.

3. Paul O'Rourke, *Blessings of the Poor* (Sydney, Australia: Strand, 2007), 68.

4. Ken Gire, *Incredible Moments with the Savior* (Grand Rapids: Zondervan Publishing House, 1990), 57.

Chapter 4

1. Tony Campolo and Gordon Aeschliman, *Everybody Wants to Change the World: Practical Ideas for Social Justice* (Ventura, Calif.: Regal Books, 2007), 25.

2. Information derived from the following two sources:

Iain Murray, *The Really Inconvenient Truths: Seven Environmental Catastrophes Liberals Don't Want You to Know About—Because They Helped Cause Them* (Washington, D.C.: Regnery Publishing, 2008).

Roy Spencer, *Climate Confusion* (New York: Encounter Books, 2008).

3. Information derived from the following three sources:

David I. Gustafson, *Reaping the Real Whirlwind: A Biblical Response to the Theory of Man-Made Global Warming* (Camp Sherman, Oreg.: VMI, 2008).

Sheryl Henderson Blunt, "Climate Change Is Here to Stay," *Christianity Today*, <http://www.ctlibrary.com/print.html?id=41730>, accessed March 2009.

Sheryl Henderson Blunt, "Cool on Climate Change," *Christianity Today*, <http://www.ctlibrary.com/print.html?id=38864>, accessed March 2009.

4. Karen Logan, *Clean House, Clean Planet* (New York: Pocket Books, 1997).

5. Anuradha Mittal, "Hunger in America," *CommonDreams.org*, December 10, 2004, <http://www.commondreams.org/views04/1210-22.htm>, accessed April 2009.

6. Donna S. Thomas, *Becoming a World Change Family: Fun and Innovative Ways to Spread the Good News* (Grand Rapids: Baker Books, 2004), 57.

Chapter 5

1. Information derived from the following three sources:

Richard Conniff, "Don't Buy Local!" *New York Times*, June 13, 2007. <http://www.newyorktimes.com>, Basic Instincts column, accessed March 2009.

"San Franciso Retail Diversity Study," *Civic Economics*, May 2007, <http://www.buylocalberkeley.com>, accessed March 2009.

Jack Hedin, "My Forbidden Fruits (and Vegetables)," *New York Times*, March 1, 2008, <http://www.newyorktimes.com >, accessed March 2009.

2. "10 Reasons to Buy Local Produce," *Growing for Market*, <http://growingformarket.com/articles/20071231>, linked from <http://www.greensgrow.org/pages_04/10reasons.html>, accessed April 2009.

3. "Buy Local Studies," <http://www.buylocalberkeley.com/node/36>, accessed March 2009.

4. E. Benjamin Skinner, "People for Sale," *UTNE*, July-August 2008.

5. Ellis Jones, *The Better World Handbook* (Gabriola Island, British Columbia: New Society Publishers, 2007), 17, 77.

6. "Let's Clean Up Fashion", Clean Clothes Campaign, <www.cleanclothes.org/lets-clean-up-fashion>, accessed May 2009.

7. <http://www.transfairusa.org/content/about/overview>, accessed April 2009.

8. <http://somd.com/news/headlines/2007/6925.shtml>, accessed April 2009.

Chapter 6

1. O'Rourke, *Blessings of the Poor*, 76.

2. Marcus Bowman of IAC Transportation, "About Your Commute: U. S. Commuting Statistics, Where Are People Going? How?" July 2008, <http://www.slideshare.net/marcus.bowman.slides/us-commuting-statistical-analysis?src=embed>, accessed February 2009.

3. "Tent Cities Rise Across the Country," Associated Press, September 18, 2008, <http://www.msnbc.msn.com/id/26776283>, accessed February 2009.

4. U. S. Department of Health and Human Services, Administration for Children and Families, "Look Beneath the Surface," Child Exploitation Brochure, <http://www.acf.hhs.gov/trafficking/about/brochures.html>, accessed April 2009.

5. "Holding the Poor Accountable," Up and Out: A Guide to True Compassion for the Poor, October 2005, <http://www.gerrycharlottephelps.com/chapter_18_holding_the_poor_accountable>, accessed January 2009.

6. Mark Vroegop, "Revealing Christ in a Recession, Mar. 15, 2009, College Park Church, <www.yourchurch.com/sermon/revealing-christ-in-a-recession>, accessed May 2009.

7. Tower Schmidt, "Art Music Justice Tour," *Relevant Magazine Online,* 2008, <http://www.relevantmagazine.com/columns/music/3893-art-music-justice-tour>, accessed April 2009.

8. Stephanie Land, *The Idealist.org Handbook to Building a Better World: How to Turn Your Good Intentions into Actions That Make a Difference* (New York: Perigee Trade, 2009).

9. Matthew Black and H. H. Rowley, *Peake's Commentary on the Bible* (London: Routledge Co. Ltd., 2001), <http://www.amazon.com/Peakes-Commentary-Bible-Matthew-Black/dp/>, accessed April 2009.

10. Robert Jamieson, A. R. Fausset, David Brown, *Commentary Critical and Explanatory of the Whole Bible,* <http://www.crosswalk.com>, accessed April 2009.

11. Pranitha Timothy, "If You Hold On, You Will Do Well," *International Justice Mission First Person,* January 9, 2009, <http://www.ijm.org/articles/firstperson>, accessed April 2009.

12. Joanna Ledgerwood, *Microfinance Handbook: An Institutional and Financial Perspective* (Washington, D. C.: The World Bank, 2000), 1.

13. Consultative Group to Assist the Poor, *Savings Services Are as Important as Credit: Deposit Services for the Poor,* CGAP Donor Brief #4, June 2002.

14. Joe Maxwell, "The Missions of Business," *Christianity Today,* November 2007.

15. Lupton, *Compassion, Justice and the Christian Life,* 121.

Chapter 7

1. *The New Testament Greek Lexicon,* <http://www.crosswalk.com>, accessed April 2009.

2. <http://en.wikipedia.org/wiki/Hospitality_ethics#References>, accessed April 2009.

3. Family Life Today, "Ten Ways Every Christian Can Care for the Orphan and Waiting Child," a resource created by Hope for Orphans®, a ministry of FamilyLife®.

4. Laura Christianson, *The Adoption Network: Your Guide to Starting a Support System* (Enumclaw, Wash.: Winepress Publishing, 2007).

Chapter 8

1. George MacDonald, *Annals of a Quiet Village,* from CD compilation by Robert Trexler (Rosley, England: Johannesen Publishers, 2006), 32.

2. Campolo and Aeschliman, *Everybody Wants to Change the World,* 127-28.
3. <http://www.slaverymap.org>, accessed April 2009).
4. "Look Beneath the Surface."

Chapter 9

1. "Volunteer Retention," Corporation for National and Community Service (April 2007), <http://www.nationalservice.gov/pdf/VIA/VIA_brief_retention.pdf>, accessed May 2009.
2. O'Rourke, *Blessings of the Poor,* 13-15.
3. John Bunyan, *The Pilgrim's Progress* (Uhrichsville, Oh.: Barbour Publishing, 1985), 44-45.

Chapter 10

1. Christian Smith and Michael O. Emerson, *Passing the Plate* (New York: Oxford University Press, 2008), 13-16.
2. Rob Moll, "Scrooge Lives!" *Christianity Today,* December 2008, 24-29.
3. Walter A. Elwell, *Evangelical Dictionary of Theology,* s.v. "tithe" and "tithing," <http://www.biblestudytools.net/Dictionaries/BakerEvangelicalDictionary/bed.cgi?number=T695, 1997>, accessed May 2009.
4. Tony Evans, "Principles of Christian Stewardship," The Urban Alternative, <http://www.tonyevans.org/site/c.feIKLOOpGlF/b.2018451/apps/s/content.asp?ct=490967>, accessed December 2008.
5. Walter A. Elwell, *Evangelical Dictionary of Theology,* s.v. "poor" and "poverty," <http://www.biblestudytools.net/Dictionaries/BakerEvangelicalDictionary/bed.cgi?number=T557, 1997>, accessed May 2009.

Chapter 11

1. Martin Hearson, "Cashing in Giant Retailers, Purchasing Practices, and Working Conditions in the Garment Industry: Executive Summary," 6, <http://cleanclothes.org/bb-news/1270-ccc-cashing-in-research-report-launched>, accessed May 2009.
2. Deepa Narayan, Robert Chambers, Meera Kaul Shah, and Patti Petesch, *Voices of the Poor: Crying Out for Change* (New York: Oxford University Press, 2000), <http://web.worldbank.org>, 236.
3. Ibid., 72.
4. Narayan et al., *Voices of the Poor,* 40.
5. Jayamma from South Asia, "I Never Dreamt of a Day like This in My Life" International Justice Mission <http://www.ijm.org/articles/firstperson-jayamma-mar2008>, accessed May 2009.
6. Narayan, Deepa with Raj Patel, Kai Schafft, Anne Rademacher and Sarah Koch-Schulte, *Voices of the Poor: Can Anyone Hear Us?* New York, N.Y.: Published for the World Bank, Oxford University Press. <http://web.worldbank.org> chapter 1, 23.
7. Bart and Linda from the Cambodian field, Free Wheel Chair Mission, The Friday Story, January 12, 2007, <http://www.freewheelchairmission.org/site/apps/

nl/newsletter2.asp?c=fgLFIXOJKtF&b=4992899&rsCount=13&recordcount=1&page=2>, accessed May 2009.

8. Luisa Nasingi, Angola, Alfalit International Inc., <http://www.alfalit.org/testimonies.html>, accessed May 2009.

9. "China—Christian Released After Two Years," Voice of the Martyrs, February 9, 2009, <http://www.persecution.com/recent_shuangShuyingRelease.html>, accessed May 2009.

10. "Geoffrey's Story," Testimonials, World Relief, <http://wer-us.org/testimonials.htm>, accessed May 2009.

11. Esther Havens and Taylor Walling, "Meet Jean Bosco", Charity Water, <http://www.charitywater.org/projects/fromthefield/rwanda.htm>, accessed May 2009.

12. "Five Latin America/Caribbean Homeowner Families," Non Pariel, Guyana, Habitat for Humanity, <http://www.habitat.org/faces_places/hom/five_homeowner_families.aspx#P0_0>, accessed May 2009.

13. Narayan, Deepa with Raj Patel, Kai Schafft, Anne Rademacher and Sarah Koch-Schulte. 2000. *Voices of the Poor: Can Anyone Hear Us?* New York, N.Y.: Published for the World Bank, Oxford University Press, <http://web.worldbank.org> chapter 7, 230.

ACKNOWLEDGMENTS

✑ "Thank you" does not seem strong enough to convey my deep gratitude for the prayers, encouragement, research, and writing help of the following group of people:

The excellent staff at Beacon Hill Press of Kansas City who made this possible: Judi Perry, Barry Russell, Bonnie Perry, Lynda Mullins, and Emily Benson.

Compassion International staff and advocate team, especially Brenda Howard, Mary Beth Wilson, and Rick Schluep, for training me and always striving for excellence.

Cynthia Ruchti and Aaron Robinson, for editing assistance.

Joe Bartemus, Dale Shaw, and Frank Pulice, for research assistance and professional expertise.

Write-to-Publish staff and my writing friends, for guiding me in the craft.

Bucky Rosenbaum, a skilled agent with a great heart.

Steve Lawson, for guidance with my initial vision.

The women I interviewed, who inspired and taught me so much.

Members of College Park Church, Grace Community Church, Horizon Christian Church, and Common Ground Church, for excellent probing conversations challenging me to clearer thinking.

Jo Pettersen, Candace Nall, Sharyn Kopf, Mindy Lerch, Jessica Dodson, Jessica Curtis, Tracey Nix, Cheryl Herndon, Carol Richhart, and Beth Olsen, along with my friends and family, for support.

My husband, Aaron, for his limitless patience and encouragement.

And Christ, my Sustainer, Protector, and Savior.

"This book inspired me with well-told stories of courageous women who changed the world and challenged me to do the same. I highly recommend it."
—Keri Wyatt Kent, author of *Breathe: Creating Space for God in a Hectic Life*

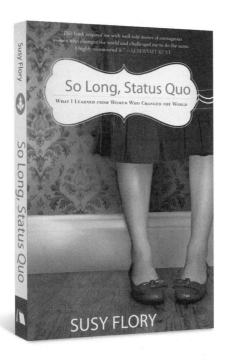

Susy Flory's life was a lot like her couch—comfortable, inviting, and safe. Then she discovered the fascinating stories of nine extraordinary women who willingly sacrificed personal comfort and convenience for a cause greater than themselves. These accounts will challenge you to examine your own life and inspire you to ask, *What can I do to get God's work done in the world?*

So Long, Status Quo
What I Learned from Women Who Changed the World
Susy Flory
ISBN: 978-0-8341-2438-7

BEACON HILL PRESS
OF KANSAS CITY

Available online or wherever books are sold.

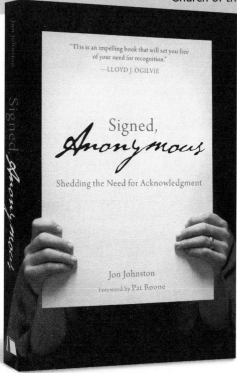
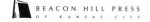

CELEBRATE GOD'S ACTIVE PRESENCE IN OUR LIVES.

With insight and inspiration, these encouraging testimonies share accounts of a loving God's divine intervention. Journey with men and women in different stages and circumstances of life as they share their stories, each full of expected and unexpected moments of God's grace, love, and mercy.

God Sightings
Stories of God's Miraculous Provision
Compiled by Joyce Williams
ISBN: 978-0-8341-2470-7

Available online or wherever books are sold.

BEACON HILL PRESS
OF KANSAS CITY